The
BOOK CLUB
journal

The
BOOK CLUB
journal

All the Books You've Read,
Loved, & Discussed

ADAMS MEDIA
New York London Toronto Sydney New Delhi

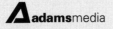

Adams Media
An Imprint of Simon & Schuster, Inc.
57 Littlefield Street
Avon, Massachusetts 02322

First Adams Media trade paperback edition October 2020

ADAMS MEDIA and colophon are trademarks of Simon & Schuster.

For information about special discounts for bulk purchases, please contact Simon & Schuster Special Sales at 1-866-506-1949 or business@simonandschuster.com.

The Simon & Schuster Speakers Bureau can bring authors to your live event. For more information or to book an event contact the Simon & Schuster Speakers Bureau at 1-866-248-3049 or visit our website at www.simonspeakers.com.

Interior design and illustrations by Priscilla Yuen
Interior images © 123RF/Angelina Chirkova, colorvalley, Dmitriy Baranov, Edwin Verin, evdakovka, kchung, Pavel Zhovba, Piotr Zajda, RIE SAKAE, sborisov, sebastien decoret, Stasyuk Stanislav, Tithi Luadthong, Wasin Pummarin

Manufactured in the United States of America

10 9 8 7 6 5 4

ISBN 978-1-5072-1402-2

CONTENTS

INTRODUCTION

Reading is an experience like no other.

You immerse yourself in a character's life and time, following the twists and turns of their journey as you flip the pages. You might find yourself feeling elated, shocked, sympathetic, thoughtful, heartbroken—after all, books can elicit every emotion. Reading a book along with a group is a powerful way to share your thoughts about the text, engage in interesting discussion, and expand your experience of the book to include other readers' perspectives.

As Charlie Jones says in *Life Is Tremendous*, "You will be the same person in five years as you are today except for the people you meet and the books you read." Books and people are powerful influencers, and a book club brings them together in an entertaining way. Whether you prefer a cerebral group held at your local library, an online group led by a celebrity, or a casual, friendly gathering at a neighbor's house, you can find a book club that matches your personality.

This journal provides a place for you to chart your thoughts about the books you read, as well as takeaways from the conversations you have around those books. The journal pages have a variety of note-taking prompts that will help you remember parts of the book that were meaningful to you, such as characters, writing style, and themes. Use the pages in a way that works for you—one person might take notes as they read; another might jot down all their thoughts after finishing the book. The My Biggest Takeaway section at the end of each entry is a spot for you to capture a simple observation like "I discovered that sci-fi isn't my preference"; "Read this book with my daughter once she turns 11"; or "I never saw my introverted nature as an asset until I read this book. I want to embrace this about myself." Write down a one- or two-sentence notation to remind, guide, or encourage your future self when you glance back through this journal.

If you're not currently part of a book club, this book also outlines how to join a club or start your own group. At the back of the book, you'll find several recommended reading lists capturing a variety of categories from classics to memoirs; sample discussion questions; and space for you to list books you want to read.

Let this journal inspire you to celebrate all the things you learn about yourself and the world around you as you read. May the journey ahead bring you joy, understanding, and wisdom!

JOURNAL
pages

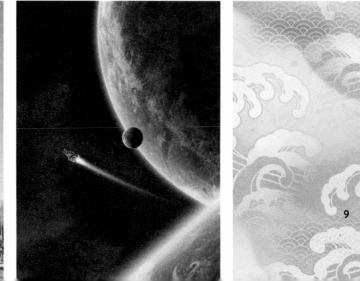

Title: ....

Author: ....

Genre: ....

Format: PAPER / DIGITAL / AUDIO

Recommended by/Why I'm reading it: ....

....

Date started: .... Date finished: ....

MY ANALYSIS

Would I read it again?   YES / NO

Would I recommend it?   YES / NO
If so, to whom? ....

....

Themes or characters that resonated with me: ....

....

Emotions, thoughts, or memories it brought up in me: ....

....

Opinion about the author or writing style: ....

....

MY RATINGS

WRITING STYLE	☆ ☆ ☆ ☆ ☆	READABILITY	☆ ☆ ☆ ☆ ☆
RELATABILITY	☆ ☆ ☆ ☆ ☆	PERSONAL IMPACT	☆ ☆ ☆ ☆ ☆
ORIGINALITY	☆ ☆ ☆ ☆ ☆	PLOT	☆ ☆ ☆ ☆ ☆
....	☆ ☆ ☆ ☆ ☆	....	☆ ☆ ☆ ☆ ☆
....	☆ ☆ ☆ ☆ ☆	....	☆ ☆ ☆ ☆ ☆
....	☆ ☆ ☆ ☆ ☆	....	☆ ☆ ☆ ☆ ☆

MY OVERALL RATING ☆ ☆ ☆ ☆ ☆

BOOK CLUB NOTES

_____

_____

_____

_____

_____

_____

_____

_____

_____

_____

_____

_____

_____

_____

_____

_____

_____

_____

_____

MY BIGGEST TAKEAWAY

_____

_____

_____

_____

_____

_____

Title: ....

Author: ....

Genre: ....

Format: PAPER / DIGITAL / AUDIO

Recommended by/Why I'm reading it: ....

....

Date started: .... Date finished: ....

MY ANALYSIS

Would I read it again?   YES / NO

Would I recommend it?   YES / NO
If so, to whom? ....

....

Themes or characters that resonated with me: ....

....

Emotions, thoughts, or memories it brought up in me: ....

....

Opinion about the author or writing style: ....

....

MY RATINGS

WRITING STYLE	☆☆☆☆☆	READABILITY	☆☆☆☆☆
RELATABILITY	☆☆☆☆☆	PERSONAL IMPACT	☆☆☆☆☆
ORIGINALITY	☆☆☆☆☆	PLOT	☆☆☆☆☆
....	☆☆☆☆☆	....	☆☆☆☆☆
....	☆☆☆☆☆	....	☆☆☆☆☆
....	☆☆☆☆☆	....	☆☆☆☆☆

MY OVERALL RATING ☆☆☆☆☆

BOOK CLUB NOTES

MY BIGGEST TAKEAWAY

Title: ....

Author: ....

Genre: ....

Format: PAPER / DIGITAL / AUDIO

Recommended by/Why I'm reading it: ....
....

Date started: .... Date finished: ....

MY ANALYSIS

Would I read it again?   YES / NO

Would I recommend it?   YES / NO
If so, to whom? ....

Themes or characters that resonated with me: ....
....

Emotions, thoughts, or memories it brought up in me: ....
....

Opinion about the author or writing style: ....
....

MY RATINGS

WRITING STYLE	☆☆☆☆☆	READABILITY	☆☆☆☆☆
RELATABILITY	☆☆☆☆☆	PERSONAL IMPACT	☆☆☆☆☆
ORIGINALITY	☆☆☆☆☆	PLOT	☆☆☆☆☆
....	☆☆☆☆☆	....	☆☆☆☆☆
....	☆☆☆☆☆	....	☆☆☆☆☆
....	☆☆☆☆☆	....	☆☆☆☆☆

MY OVERALL RATING ☆☆☆☆☆

BOOK CLUB NOTES

MY BIGGEST TAKEAWAY

Title: ....

Author: ....

Genre: ....

Format: PAPER / DIGITAL / AUDIO

Recommended by/Why I'm reading it: ....
....

Date started: ....   Date finished: ....

MY ANALYSIS

Would I read it again?   YES / NO

Would I recommend it?   YES / NO
If so, to whom? ....
....

Themes or characters that resonated with me: ....
....

Emotions, thoughts, or memories it brought up in me: ....
....

Opinion about the author or writing style: ....
....

MY RATINGS

WRITING STYLE	☆☆☆☆☆	READABILITY	☆☆☆☆☆
RELATABILITY	☆☆☆☆☆	PERSONAL IMPACT	☆☆☆☆☆
ORIGINALITY	☆☆☆☆☆	PLOT	☆☆☆☆☆
....	☆☆☆☆☆	....	☆☆☆☆☆
....	☆☆☆☆☆	....	☆☆☆☆☆
....	☆☆☆☆☆	....	☆☆☆☆☆

MY OVERALL RATING ☆☆☆☆☆

BOOK CLUB NOTES

MY BIGGEST TAKEAWAY

Title: ....

Author: ....

Genre: ....

Format: PAPER / DIGITAL / AUDIO

Recommended by/Why I'm reading it: ....

....

Date started: .... Date finished: ....

MY ANALYSIS

Would I read it again?   YES / NO

Would I recommend it?   YES / NO

If so, to whom? ....

....

Themes or characters that resonated with me: ....

....

Emotions, thoughts, or memories it brought up in me: ....

....

Opinion about the author or writing style: ....

....

MY RATINGS

WRITING STYLE	☆☆☆☆☆	READABILITY	☆☆☆☆☆
RELATABILITY	☆☆☆☆☆	PERSONAL IMPACT	☆☆☆☆☆
ORIGINALITY	☆☆☆☆☆	PLOT	☆☆☆☆☆
....	☆☆☆☆☆	....	☆☆☆☆☆
....	☆☆☆☆☆	....	☆☆☆☆☆
....	☆☆☆☆☆	....	☆☆☆☆☆

MY OVERALL RATING ☆☆☆☆☆

BOOK CLUB NOTES

MY BIGGEST TAKEAWAY

Title: ....

Author: ....

Genre: ....

Format: PAPER / DIGITAL / AUDIO

Recommended by/Why I'm reading it: ....

....

Date started: .... Date finished: ....

MY ANALYSIS

Would I read it again?   YES / NO

Would I recommend it?   YES / NO

If so, to whom? ....

....

Themes or characters that resonated with me: ....

....

Emotions, thoughts, or memories it brought up in me: ....

....

Opinion about the author or writing style: ....

....

MY RATINGS

WRITING STYLE	☆☆☆☆☆	READABILITY	☆☆☆☆☆
RELATABILITY	☆☆☆☆☆	PERSONAL IMPACT	☆☆☆☆☆
ORIGINALITY	☆☆☆☆☆	PLOT	☆☆☆☆☆
....	☆☆☆☆☆	....	☆☆☆☆☆
....	☆☆☆☆☆	....	☆☆☆☆☆
....	☆☆☆☆☆	....	☆☆☆☆☆

MY OVERALL RATING ☆☆☆☆☆

BOOK CLUB NOTES

MY BIGGEST TAKEAWAY

Title: ....

Author: ....

Genre: ....

Format: PAPER / DIGITAL / AUDIO

Recommended by/Why I'm reading it: ....

....

Date started: .... Date finished: ....

MY ANALYSIS

Would I read it again?   YES / NO

Would I recommend it?   YES / NO

If so, to whom? ....

....

Themes or characters that resonated with me: ....

....

Emotions, thoughts, or memories it brought up in me: ....

....

Opinion about the author or writing style: ....

....

MY RATINGS

WRITING STYLE	☆☆☆☆☆	READABILITY	☆☆☆☆☆
RELATABILITY	☆☆☆☆☆	PERSONAL IMPACT	☆☆☆☆☆
ORIGINALITY	☆☆☆☆☆	PLOT	☆☆☆☆☆
....	☆☆☆☆☆	....	☆☆☆☆☆
....	☆☆☆☆☆	....	☆☆☆☆☆
....	☆☆☆☆☆	....	☆☆☆☆☆

MY OVERALL RATING ☆☆☆☆☆

BOOK CLUB NOTES

MY BIGGEST TAKEAWAY

Title: ....

Author: ....

Genre: ....

Format: PAPER / DIGITAL / AUDIO

Recommended by/Why I'm reading it: ....

....

Date started: .... Date finished: ....

MY ANALYSIS

Would I read it again?   YES / NO

Would I recommend it?   YES / NO

If so, to whom? ....

....

Themes or characters that resonated with me: ....

....

Emotions, thoughts, or memories it brought up in me: ....

....

Opinion about the author or writing style: ....

....

MY RATINGS

WRITING STYLE	☆☆☆☆☆	READABILITY	☆☆☆☆☆
RELATABILITY	☆☆☆☆☆	PERSONAL IMPACT	☆☆☆☆☆
ORIGINALITY	☆☆☆☆☆	PLOT	☆☆☆☆☆
....	☆☆☆☆☆	....	☆☆☆☆☆
....	☆☆☆☆☆	....	☆☆☆☆☆
....	☆☆☆☆☆	....	☆☆☆☆☆

MY OVERALL RATING ☆☆☆☆☆

BOOK CLUB NOTES

MY BIGGEST TAKEAWAY

Title: ....

Author: ....

Genre: ....

Format: PAPER / DIGITAL / AUDIO

Recommended by/Why I'm reading it: ....
....

Date started: .... Date finished: ....

MY ANALYSIS

Would I read it again?   YES / NO

Would I recommend it?   YES / NO
If so, to whom? ....
....

Themes or characters that resonated with me: ....
....

Emotions, thoughts, or memories it brought up in me: .....
....

Opinion about the author or writing style: ....
....

MY RATINGS

WRITING STYLE	☆ ☆ ☆ ☆ ☆	READABILITY	☆ ☆ ☆ ☆ ☆
RELATABILITY	☆ ☆ ☆ ☆ ☆	PERSONAL IMPACT	☆ ☆ ☆ ☆ ☆
ORIGINALITY	☆ ☆ ☆ ☆ ☆	PLOT	☆ ☆ ☆ ☆ ☆
....	☆ ☆ ☆ ☆ ☆	....	☆ ☆ ☆ ☆ ☆
....	☆ ☆ ☆ ☆ ☆	....	☆ ☆ ☆ ☆ ☆
....	☆ ☆ ☆ ☆ ☆	....	☆ ☆ ☆ ☆ ☆

MY OVERALL RATING ☆ ☆ ☆ ☆ ☆

BOOK CLUB NOTES

MY BIGGEST TAKEAWAY

Title: ....

Author: ....

Genre: ....

Format: PAPER / DIGITAL / AUDIO

Recommended by/Why I'm reading it: ....

....

Date started: .... Date finished: ....

MY ANALYSIS

Would I read it again?   YES / NO

Would I recommend it?   YES / NO
If so, to whom? ....

....

Themes or characters that resonated with me: ....

....

Emotions, thoughts, or memories it brought up in me: ....

....

Opinion about the author or writing style: ....

....

MY RATINGS

WRITING STYLE	☆ ☆ ☆ ☆ ☆	READABILITY	☆ ☆ ☆ ☆ ☆
RELATABILITY	☆ ☆ ☆ ☆ ☆	PERSONAL IMPACT	☆ ☆ ☆ ☆ ☆
ORIGINALITY	☆ ☆ ☆ ☆ ☆	PLOT	☆ ☆ ☆ ☆ ☆
....	☆ ☆ ☆ ☆ ☆	....	☆ ☆ ☆ ☆ ☆
....	☆ ☆ ☆ ☆ ☆	....	☆ ☆ ☆ ☆ ☆
....	☆ ☆ ☆ ☆ ☆	....	☆ ☆ ☆ ☆ ☆

MY OVERALL RATING   ☆ ☆ ☆ ☆ ☆

BOOK CLUB NOTES

MY BIGGEST TAKEAWAY

Title: ....

Author: ....

Genre: ....

Format: PAPER / DIGITAL / AUDIO

Recommended by/Why I'm reading it: ....

....

Date started: .... Date finished: ....

MY ANALYSIS

Would I read it again?   YES / NO

Would I recommend it?   YES / NO
If so, to whom? ....

....

Themes or characters that resonated with me: ....

....

Emotions, thoughts, or memories it brought up in me: ....

....

Opinion about the author or writing style: ....

....

MY RATINGS

WRITING STYLE	☆ ☆ ☆ ☆ ☆	READABILITY	☆ ☆ ☆ ☆ ☆
RELATABILITY	☆ ☆ ☆ ☆ ☆	PERSONAL IMPACT	☆ ☆ ☆ ☆ ☆
ORIGINALITY	☆ ☆ ☆ ☆ ☆	PLOT	☆ ☆ ☆ ☆ ☆
....	☆ ☆ ☆ ☆ ☆	....	☆ ☆ ☆ ☆ ☆
....	☆ ☆ ☆ ☆ ☆	....	☆ ☆ ☆ ☆ ☆
....	☆ ☆ ☆ ☆ ☆	....	☆ ☆ ☆ ☆ ☆

MY OVERALL RATING ☆ ☆ ☆ ☆ ☆

BOOK CLUB NOTES

MY BIGGEST TAKEAWAY

Title: ....

Author: ....

Genre: ....

Format: PAPER / DIGITAL / AUDIO

Recommended by/Why I'm reading it: ....
....

Date started: ....   Date finished: ....

MY ANALYSIS

Would I read it again?   YES / NO

Would I recommend it?   YES / NO
If so, to whom? ....
....

Themes or characters that resonated with me: ....
....

Emotions, thoughts, or memories it brought up in me: ....
....

Opinion about the author or writing style: ....
....

MY RATINGS

WRITING STYLE	☆ ☆ ☆ ☆ ☆	READABILITY	☆ ☆ ☆ ☆ ☆
RELATABILITY	☆ ☆ ☆ ☆ ☆	PERSONAL IMPACT	☆ ☆ ☆ ☆ ☆
ORIGINALITY	☆ ☆ ☆ ☆ ☆	PLOT	☆ ☆ ☆ ☆ ☆
....	☆ ☆ ☆ ☆ ☆	....	☆ ☆ ☆ ☆ ☆
....	☆ ☆ ☆ ☆ ☆	....	☆ ☆ ☆ ☆ ☆
....	☆ ☆ ☆ ☆ ☆	....	☆ ☆ ☆ ☆ ☆

MY OVERALL RATING ☆ ☆ ☆ ☆ ☆

BOOK CLUB NOTES

MY BIGGEST TAKEAWAY

Title: ....

Author: ....

Genre: ....

Format: PAPER / DIGITAL / AUDIO

Recommended by/Why I'm reading it: ....

....

Date started: .... Date finished: ....

MY ANALYSIS

Would I read it again?   YES / NO

Would I recommend it?   YES / NO

If so, to whom? ....

....

Themes or characters that resonated with me: ....

....

Emotions, thoughts, or memories it brought up in me: ....

....

Opinion about the author or writing style: ....

....

MY RATINGS

WRITING STYLE	☆ ☆ ☆ ☆ ☆	READABILITY	☆ ☆ ☆ ☆ ☆
RELATABILITY	☆ ☆ ☆ ☆ ☆	PERSONAL IMPACT	☆ ☆ ☆ ☆ ☆
ORIGINALITY	☆ ☆ ☆ ☆ ☆	PLOT	☆ ☆ ☆ ☆ ☆
....	☆ ☆ ☆ ☆ ☆	....	☆ ☆ ☆ ☆ ☆
....	☆ ☆ ☆ ☆ ☆	....	☆ ☆ ☆ ☆ ☆
....	☆ ☆ ☆ ☆ ☆	....	☆ ☆ ☆ ☆ ☆

MY OVERALL RATING   ☆ ☆ ☆ ☆ ☆

BOOK CLUB NOTES

MY BIGGEST TAKEAWAY

Title: ....

Author: ....

Genre: ....

Format: PAPER / DIGITAL / AUDIO

Recommended by/Why I'm reading it: ....

....

Date started: .... Date finished: ....

MY ANALYSIS

Would I read it again?   YES / NO

Would I recommend it?   YES / NO

If so, to whom? ....

....

Themes or characters that resonated with me: ....

....

Emotions, thoughts, or memories it brought up in me: ....

....

Opinion about the author or writing style: ....

....

MY RATINGS

WRITING STYLE	☆☆☆☆☆	READABILITY	☆☆☆☆☆
RELATABILITY	☆☆☆☆☆	PERSONAL IMPACT	☆☆☆☆☆
ORIGINALITY	☆☆☆☆☆	PLOT	☆☆☆☆☆
....	☆☆☆☆☆	....	☆☆☆☆☆
....	☆☆☆☆☆	....	☆☆☆☆☆
....	☆☆☆☆☆	....	☆☆☆☆☆

MY OVERALL RATING ☆☆☆☆☆

BOOK CLUB NOTES

....
....
....
....
....
....
....
....
....
....
....
....
....
....
....
....
....

MY BIGGEST TAKEAWAY

....
....
....
....
....

Title: ....

Author: ....

Genre: ....

Format: PAPER / DIGITAL / AUDIO

Recommended by/Why I'm reading it: ....

....

Date started: .... Date finished: ....

MY ANALYSIS

Would I read it again?   YES / NO

Would I recommend it?   YES / NO
If so, to whom? ....

....

Themes or characters that resonated with me: ....

....

Emotions, thoughts, or memories it brought up in me: ....

....

Opinion about the author or writing style: ....

....

MY RATINGS

WRITING STYLE	☆ ☆ ☆ ☆ ☆	READABILITY	☆ ☆ ☆ ☆ ☆
RELATABILITY	☆ ☆ ☆ ☆ ☆	PERSONAL IMPACT	☆ ☆ ☆ ☆ ☆
ORIGINALITY	☆ ☆ ☆ ☆ ☆	PLOT	☆ ☆ ☆ ☆ ☆
....	☆ ☆ ☆ ☆ ☆	....	☆ ☆ ☆ ☆ ☆
....	☆ ☆ ☆ ☆ ☆	....	☆ ☆ ☆ ☆ ☆
....	☆ ☆ ☆ ☆ ☆	....	☆ ☆ ☆ ☆ ☆

MY OVERALL RATING ☆ ☆ ☆ ☆ ☆

BOOK CLUB NOTES

MY BIGGEST TAKEAWAY

Title: ....

Author: ....

Genre: ....

Format: PAPER / DIGITAL / AUDIO

Recommended by/Why I'm reading it: ....
....

Date started: .... Date finished: ....

MY ANALYSIS

Would I read it again?   YES / NO

Would I recommend it?   YES / NO
If so, to whom? ....
....

Themes or characters that resonated with me: ....
....

Emotions, thoughts, or memories it brought up in me: ....
....

Opinion about the author or writing style: ....
....

MY RATINGS

WRITING STYLE	☆ ☆ ☆ ☆ ☆	READABILITY	☆ ☆ ☆ ☆ ☆
RELATABILITY	☆ ☆ ☆ ☆ ☆	PERSONAL IMPACT	☆ ☆ ☆ ☆ ☆
ORIGINALITY	☆ ☆ ☆ ☆ ☆	PLOT	☆ ☆ ☆ ☆ ☆
....	☆ ☆ ☆ ☆ ☆	....	☆ ☆ ☆ ☆ ☆
....	☆ ☆ ☆ ☆ ☆	....	☆ ☆ ☆ ☆ ☆
....	☆ ☆ ☆ ☆ ☆	....	☆ ☆ ☆ ☆ ☆

MY OVERALL RATING ☆ ☆ ☆ ☆ ☆

BOOK CLUB NOTES

MY BIGGEST TAKEAWAY

Title: ....

Author: ....

Genre: ....

Format: PAPER / DIGITAL / AUDIO

Recommended by/Why I'm reading it: ....

....

Date started: .... Date finished: ....

MY ANALYSIS

Would I read it again?   YES / NO

Would I recommend it?   YES / NO

If so, to whom? ....

....

Themes or characters that resonated with me: ....

....

Emotions, thoughts, or memories it brought up in me: ....

....

Opinion about the author or writing style: ....

....

MY RATINGS

WRITING STYLE	☆☆☆☆☆	READABILITY	☆☆☆☆☆
RELATABILITY	☆☆☆☆☆	PERSONAL IMPACT	☆☆☆☆☆
ORIGINALITY	☆☆☆☆☆	PLOT	☆☆☆☆☆
....	☆☆☆☆☆	....	☆☆☆☆☆
....	☆☆☆☆☆	....	☆☆☆☆☆
....	☆☆☆☆☆	....	☆☆☆☆☆

MY OVERALL RATING ☆☆☆☆☆

BOOK CLUB NOTES

MY BIGGEST TAKEAWAY

Title: ....

Author: ....

Genre: ....

Format: PAPER / DIGITAL / AUDIO

Recommended by/Why I'm reading it: ....

....

Date started: .... Date finished: ....

MY ANALYSIS

Would I read it again? YES / NO

Would I recommend it? YES / NO

If so, to whom? ....

....

Themes or characters that resonated with me: ....

....

Emotions, thoughts, or memories it brought up in me: ....

....

Opinion about the author or writing style: ....

....

MY RATINGS

WRITING STYLE	☆☆☆☆☆	READABILITY	☆☆☆☆☆
RELATABILITY	☆☆☆☆☆	PERSONAL IMPACT	☆☆☆☆☆
ORIGINALITY	☆☆☆☆☆	PLOT	☆☆☆☆☆
....	☆☆☆☆☆	....	☆☆☆☆☆
....	☆☆☆☆☆	....	☆☆☆☆☆
....	☆☆☆☆☆	....	☆☆☆☆☆

MY OVERALL RATING ☆☆☆☆☆

BOOK CLUB NOTES

MY BIGGEST TAKEAWAY

Title: ....

Author: ....

Genre: ....

Format: PAPER / DIGITAL / AUDIO

Recommended by/Why I'm reading it: ....

....

Date started: .... Date finished: ....

MY ANALYSIS

Would I read it again?   YES / NO

Would I recommend it?   YES / NO
If so, to whom? ....

....

Themes or characters that resonated with me: ....

....

Emotions, thoughts, or memories it brought up in me: ....

....

Opinion about the author or writing style: ....

....

MY RATINGS

WRITING STYLE	☆ ☆ ☆ ☆ ☆	READABILITY	☆ ☆ ☆ ☆ ☆
RELATABILITY	☆ ☆ ☆ ☆ ☆	PERSONAL IMPACT	☆ ☆ ☆ ☆ ☆
ORIGINALITY	☆ ☆ ☆ ☆ ☆	PLOT	☆ ☆ ☆ ☆ ☆
....	☆ ☆ ☆ ☆ ☆	....	☆ ☆ ☆ ☆ ☆
....	☆ ☆ ☆ ☆ ☆	....	☆ ☆ ☆ ☆ ☆
....	☆ ☆ ☆ ☆ ☆	....	☆ ☆ ☆ ☆ ☆

MY OVERALL RATING ☆ ☆ ☆ ☆ ☆

BOOK CLUB NOTES

MY BIGGEST TAKEAWAY

Title: ....

Author: ....

Genre: ....

Format: PAPER / DIGITAL / AUDIO

Recommended by/Why I'm reading it: ....

....

Date started: .... Date finished: ....

MY ANALYSIS

Would I read it again?   YES / NO

Would I recommend it?   YES / NO

If so, to whom? ....

....

Themes or characters that resonated with me: ....

....

Emotions, thoughts, or memories it brought up in me: ....

....

Opinion about the author or writing style: ....

....

MY RATINGS

WRITING STYLE	☆ ☆ ☆ ☆ ☆	READABILITY	☆ ☆ ☆ ☆ ☆
RELATABILITY	☆ ☆ ☆ ☆ ☆	PERSONAL IMPACT	☆ ☆ ☆ ☆ ☆
ORIGINALITY	☆ ☆ ☆ ☆ ☆	PLOT	☆ ☆ ☆ ☆ ☆
....	☆ ☆ ☆ ☆ ☆	....	☆ ☆ ☆ ☆ ☆
....	☆ ☆ ☆ ☆ ☆	....	☆ ☆ ☆ ☆ ☆
....	☆ ☆ ☆ ☆ ☆	....	☆ ☆ ☆ ☆ ☆

MY OVERALL RATING ☆ ☆ ☆ ☆ ☆

BOOK CLUB NOTES

MY BIGGEST TAKEAWAY

Title: ....

Author: ....

Genre: ....

Format: PAPER / DIGITAL / AUDIO

Recommended by/Why I'm reading it: ....

....

Date started: .... Date finished: ....

MY ANALYSIS

Would I read it again?   YES / NO

Would I recommend it?   YES / NO

If so, to whom? ....

....

Themes or characters that resonated with me: ....

....

Emotions, thoughts, or memories it brought up in me: ....

....

Opinion about the author or writing style: ....

....

MY RATINGS

WRITING STYLE	☆ ☆ ☆ ☆ ☆	READABILITY	☆ ☆ ☆ ☆ ☆
RELATABILITY	☆ ☆ ☆ ☆ ☆	PERSONAL IMPACT	☆ ☆ ☆ ☆ ☆
ORIGINALITY	☆ ☆ ☆ ☆ ☆	PLOT	☆ ☆ ☆ ☆ ☆
....	☆ ☆ ☆ ☆ ☆	....	☆ ☆ ☆ ☆ ☆
....	☆ ☆ ☆ ☆ ☆	....	☆ ☆ ☆ ☆ ☆
....	☆ ☆ ☆ ☆ ☆	....	☆ ☆ ☆ ☆ ☆

MY OVERALL RATING ☆ ☆ ☆ ☆ ☆

BOOK CLUB NOTES

MY BIGGEST TAKEAWAY

Title: ....

Author: ....

Genre: ....

Format: PAPER / DIGITAL / AUDIO

Recommended by/Why I'm reading it: ....

....

Date started: .... Date finished: ....

MY ANALYSIS

Would I read it again?   YES / NO

Would I recommend it?   YES / NO

If so, to whom? ....

....

Themes or characters that resonated with me: ....

....

Emotions, thoughts, or memories it brought up in me: ....

....

Opinion about the author or writing style: ....

....

MY RATINGS

WRITING STYLE	☆☆☆☆☆	READABILITY	☆☆☆☆☆
RELATABILITY	☆☆☆☆☆	PERSONAL IMPACT	☆☆☆☆☆
ORIGINALITY	☆☆☆☆☆	PLOT	☆☆☆☆☆
....	☆☆☆☆☆	....	☆☆☆☆☆
....	☆☆☆☆☆	....	☆☆☆☆☆
....	☆☆☆☆☆	....	☆☆☆☆☆

MY OVERALL RATING ☆☆☆☆☆

BOOK CLUB NOTES

MY BIGGEST TAKEAWAY

Title: ....

Author: ....

Genre: ....

Format: PAPER / DIGITAL / AUDIO

Recommended by/Why I'm reading it: ....

....

Date started: .... Date finished: ....

MY ANALYSIS

Would I read it again?   YES / NO

Would I recommend it?   YES / NO
If so, to whom? ....

....

Themes or characters that resonated with me: ....

....

Emotions, thoughts, or memories it brought up in me: ....

....

Opinion about the author or writing style: ....

....

MY RATINGS

WRITING STYLE	☆ ☆ ☆ ☆ ☆	READABILITY	☆ ☆ ☆ ☆ ☆
RELATABILITY	☆ ☆ ☆ ☆ ☆	PERSONAL IMPACT	☆ ☆ ☆ ☆ ☆
ORIGINALITY	☆ ☆ ☆ ☆ ☆	PLOT	☆ ☆ ☆ ☆ ☆
....	☆ ☆ ☆ ☆ ☆	....	☆ ☆ ☆ ☆ ☆
....	☆ ☆ ☆ ☆ ☆	....	☆ ☆ ☆ ☆ ☆
....	☆ ☆ ☆ ☆ ☆	....	☆ ☆ ☆ ☆ ☆

MY OVERALL RATING ☆ ☆ ☆ ☆ ☆

BOOK CLUB NOTES

MY BIGGEST TAKEAWAY

Title: ....

Author: ....

Genre: ....

Format: PAPER / DIGITAL / AUDIO

Recommended by/Why I'm reading it: ....
....

Date started: .... Date finished: ....

MY ANALYSIS

Would I read it again?   YES / NO

Would I recommend it?   YES / NO
If so, to whom? ....
....

Themes or characters that resonated with me: ....
....

Emotions, thoughts, or memories it brought up in me: ......
....

Opinion about the author or writing style: ....
....

MY RATINGS

WRITING STYLE	☆☆☆☆☆	READABILITY ☆☆☆☆☆
RELATABILITY	☆☆☆☆☆	PERSONAL IMPACT ☆☆☆☆☆
ORIGINALITY	☆☆☆☆☆	PLOT ☆☆☆☆☆
....	☆☆☆☆☆	.... ☆☆☆☆☆
....	☆☆☆☆☆	.... ☆☆☆☆☆
....	☆☆☆☆☆	.... ☆☆☆☆☆

MY OVERALL RATING ☆☆☆☆☆

BOOK CLUB NOTES

MY BIGGEST TAKEAWAY

Title: ....

Author: ....

Genre: ....

Format: PAPER / DIGITAL / AUDIO

Recommended by/Why I'm reading it: ....
....

Date started: .... Date finished: ....

MY ANALYSIS

Would I read it again?   YES / NO

Would I recommend it?   YES / NO

If so, to whom? ....
....

Themes or characters that resonated with me: ....
....

Emotions, thoughts, or memories it brought up in me: ....
....

Opinion about the author or writing style: ....
....

MY RATINGS

WRITING STYLE	☆ ☆ ☆ ☆ ☆	READABILITY	☆ ☆ ☆ ☆ ☆
RELATABILITY	☆ ☆ ☆ ☆ ☆	PERSONAL IMPACT	☆ ☆ ☆ ☆ ☆
ORIGINALITY	☆ ☆ ☆ ☆ ☆	PLOT	☆ ☆ ☆ ☆ ☆
....	☆ ☆ ☆ ☆ ☆	....	☆ ☆ ☆ ☆ ☆
....	☆ ☆ ☆ ☆ ☆	....	☆ ☆ ☆ ☆ ☆
....	☆ ☆ ☆ ☆ ☆	....	☆ ☆ ☆ ☆ ☆

MY OVERALL RATING ☆ ☆ ☆ ☆ ☆

BOOK CLUB NOTES

MY BIGGEST TAKEAWAY

Title: ....

Author: ....

Genre: ....

Format: PAPER / DIGITAL / AUDIO

Recommended by/Why I'm reading it: ....

....

Date started: ....   Date finished: ....

MY ANALYSIS

Would I read it again?   YES / NO

Would I recommend it?   YES / NO
If so, to whom? ....

....

Themes or characters that resonated with me: ....

....

Emotions, thoughts, or memories it brought up in me: ....

....

Opinion about the author or writing style: ....

....

MY RATINGS

WRITING STYLE	☆ ☆ ☆ ☆ ☆	READABILITY	☆ ☆ ☆ ☆ ☆
RELATABILITY	☆ ☆ ☆ ☆ ☆	PERSONAL IMPACT	☆ ☆ ☆ ☆ ☆
ORIGINALITY	☆ ☆ ☆ ☆ ☆	PLOT	☆ ☆ ☆ ☆ ☆
....	☆ ☆ ☆ ☆ ☆	....	☆ ☆ ☆ ☆ ☆
....	☆ ☆ ☆ ☆ ☆	....	☆ ☆ ☆ ☆ ☆
....	☆ ☆ ☆ ☆ ☆	....	☆ ☆ ☆ ☆ ☆

MY OVERALL RATING   ☆ ☆ ☆ ☆ ☆

BOOK CLUB NOTES

....
....
....
....
....
....
....
....
....
....
....
....
....
....
....
....
....
....

MY BIGGEST TAKEAWAY

....
....
....
....
....

Title: ....

Author: ....

Genre: ....

Format: PAPER / DIGITAL / AUDIO

Recommended by/Why I'm reading it: ....
....

Date started: ....   Date finished: ....

MY ANALYSIS

Would I read it again?   YES / NO

Would I recommend it?   YES / NO
If so, to whom? ....
....

Themes or characters that resonated with me: ....
....

Emotions, thoughts, or memories it brought up in me: ....
....

Opinion about the author or writing style: ....
....

MY RATINGS

WRITING STYLE	☆ ☆ ☆ ☆ ☆	READABILITY	☆ ☆ ☆ ☆ ☆
RELATABILITY	☆ ☆ ☆ ☆ ☆	PERSONAL IMPACT	☆ ☆ ☆ ☆ ☆
ORIGINALITY	☆ ☆ ☆ ☆ ☆	PLOT	☆ ☆ ☆ ☆ ☆
....	☆ ☆ ☆ ☆ ☆	....	☆ ☆ ☆ ☆ ☆
....	☆ ☆ ☆ ☆ ☆	....	☆ ☆ ☆ ☆ ☆
....	☆ ☆ ☆ ☆ ☆	....	☆ ☆ ☆ ☆ ☆

MY OVERALL RATING   ☆ ☆ ☆ ☆ ☆

BOOK CLUB NOTES

MY BIGGEST TAKEAWAY

Title: ....

Author: ....

Genre: ....

Format: PAPER / DIGITAL / AUDIO

Recommended by/Why I'm reading it: ....

....

Date started: .... Date finished: ....

MY ANALYSIS

Would I read it again?   YES / NO

Would I recommend it?   YES / NO
If so, to whom? ....

Themes or characters that resonated with me: ....

....

Emotions, thoughts, or memories it brought up in me: ....

....

Opinion about the author or writing style: ....

....

MY RATINGS

WRITING STYLE	☆☆☆☆☆	READABILITY	☆☆☆☆☆
RELATABILITY	☆☆☆☆☆	PERSONAL IMPACT	☆☆☆☆☆
ORIGINALITY	☆☆☆☆☆	PLOT	☆☆☆☆☆
....	☆☆☆☆☆	....	☆☆☆☆☆
....	☆☆☆☆☆	....	☆☆☆☆☆
....	☆☆☆☆☆	....	☆☆☆☆☆

MY OVERALL RATING ☆☆☆☆☆

BOOK CLUB NOTES

MY BIGGEST TAKEAWAY

Title: ....

Author: ....

Genre: ....

Format: PAPER / DIGITAL / AUDIO

Recommended by/Why I'm reading it: ....

....

Date started: .... Date finished: ....

MY ANALYSIS

Would I read it again?   YES / NO

Would I recommend it?   YES / NO

If so, to whom? ....

....

Themes or characters that resonated with me: ....

....

Emotions, thoughts, or memories it brought up in me: ....

....

Opinion about the author or writing style: ....

....

MY RATINGS

WRITING STYLE	☆☆☆☆☆	READABILITY	☆☆☆☆☆
RELATABILITY	☆☆☆☆☆	PERSONAL IMPACT	☆☆☆☆☆
ORIGINALITY	☆☆☆☆☆	PLOT	☆☆☆☆☆
....	☆☆☆☆☆	....	☆☆☆☆☆
....	☆☆☆☆☆	....	☆☆☆☆☆
....	☆☆☆☆☆	....	☆☆☆☆☆

MY OVERALL RATING ☆☆☆☆☆

BOOK CLUB NOTES

MY BIGGEST TAKEAWAY

Title: ....

Author: ....

Genre: ....

Format: PAPER / DIGITAL / AUDIO

Recommended by/Why I'm reading it: ....

....

Date started: ....   Date finished: ....

MY ANALYSIS

Would I read it again?   YES / NO

Would I recommend it?   YES / NO

If so, to whom? ....

....

Themes or characters that resonated with me: ....

....

Emotions, thoughts, or memories it brought up in me: ....

....

Opinion about the author or writing style: ....

....

MY RATINGS

WRITING STYLE	☆☆☆☆☆	READABILITY	☆☆☆☆☆
RELATABILITY	☆☆☆☆☆	PERSONAL IMPACT	☆☆☆☆☆
ORIGINALITY	☆☆☆☆☆	PLOT	☆☆☆☆☆
....	☆☆☆☆☆	....	☆☆☆☆☆
....	☆☆☆☆☆	....	☆☆☆☆☆
....	☆☆☆☆☆	....	☆☆☆☆☆

MY OVERALL RATING ☆☆☆☆☆

BOOK CLUB NOTES

MY BIGGEST TAKEAWAY

Title: ....

Author: ....

Genre: ....

Format: PAPER / DIGITAL / AUDIO

Recommended by/Why I'm reading it: ....

....

Date started: ....   Date finished: ....

MY ANALYSIS

Would I read it again?   YES / NO

Would I recommend it?   YES / NO

If so, to whom? ....

....

Themes or characters that resonated with me: ....

....

Emotions, thoughts, or memories it brought up in me: ....

....

Opinion about the author or writing style: ....

....

MY RATINGS

WRITING STYLE	☆ ☆ ☆ ☆ ☆	READABILITY	☆ ☆ ☆ ☆ ☆
RELATABILITY	☆ ☆ ☆ ☆ ☆	PERSONAL IMPACT	☆ ☆ ☆ ☆ ☆
ORIGINALITY	☆ ☆ ☆ ☆ ☆	PLOT	☆ ☆ ☆ ☆ ☆
....	☆ ☆ ☆ ☆ ☆	....	☆ ☆ ☆ ☆ ☆
....	☆ ☆ ☆ ☆ ☆	....	☆ ☆ ☆ ☆ ☆
....	☆ ☆ ☆ ☆ ☆	....	☆ ☆ ☆ ☆ ☆

MY OVERALL RATING ☆ ☆ ☆ ☆ ☆

BOOK CLUB NOTES

MY BIGGEST TAKEAWAY

Title: ....

Author: ....

Genre: ....

Format: PAPER / DIGITAL / AUDIO

Recommended by/Why I'm reading it: ....

....

Date started: ....   Date finished: ....

MY ANALYSIS

Would I read it again?   YES / NO

Would I recommend it?   YES / NO
If so, to whom? ....

....

Themes or characters that resonated with me: ....

....

Emotions, thoughts, or memories it brought up in me: ......

....

Opinion about the author or writing style: ....

....

MY RATINGS

WRITING STYLE	☆☆☆☆☆	READABILITY	☆☆☆☆☆
RELATABILITY	☆☆☆☆☆	PERSONAL IMPACT	☆☆☆☆☆
ORIGINALITY	☆☆☆☆☆	PLOT	☆☆☆☆☆
....	☆☆☆☆☆	....	☆☆☆☆☆
....	☆☆☆☆☆	....	☆☆☆☆☆
....	☆☆☆☆☆	....	☆☆☆☆☆

MY OVERALL RATING ☆☆☆☆☆

BOOK CLUB NOTES

MY BIGGEST TAKEAWAY

Title: ....

Author: ....

Genre: ....

Format: PAPER / DIGITAL / AUDIO

Recommended by/Why I'm reading it: ....

....

Date started: .... Date finished: ....

MY ANALYSIS

Would I read it again? YES / NO

Would I recommend it? YES / NO

If so, to whom? ....

....

Themes or characters that resonated with me: ....

....

Emotions, thoughts, or memories it brought up in me: ....

....

Opinion about the author or writing style: ....

....

MY RATINGS

WRITING STYLE	☆☆☆☆☆	READABILITY	☆☆☆☆☆
RELATABILITY	☆☆☆☆☆	PERSONAL IMPACT	☆☆☆☆☆
ORIGINALITY	☆☆☆☆☆	PLOT	☆☆☆☆☆
....	☆☆☆☆☆	....	☆☆☆☆☆
....	☆☆☆☆☆	....	☆☆☆☆☆
....	☆☆☆☆☆	....	☆☆☆☆☆

MY OVERALL RATING ☆☆☆☆☆

BOOK CLUB NOTES

MY BIGGEST TAKEAWAY

Title: ....

Author: ....

Genre: ....

Format: PAPER / DIGITAL / AUDIO

Recommended by/Why I'm reading it: ....

....

Date started: .... Date finished: ....

MY ANALYSIS

Would I read it again?   YES / NO

Would I recommend it?   YES / NO
If so, to whom? ....

....

Themes or characters that resonated with me: ....

....

Emotions, thoughts, or memories it brought up in me: ....

....

Opinion about the author or writing style: ....

....

MY RATINGS

WRITING STYLE	☆☆☆☆☆	READABILITY	☆☆☆☆☆
RELATABILITY	☆☆☆☆☆	PERSONAL IMPACT	☆☆☆☆☆
ORIGINALITY	☆☆☆☆☆	PLOT	☆☆☆☆☆
....	☆☆☆☆☆	....	☆☆☆☆☆
....	☆☆☆☆☆	....	☆☆☆☆☆
....	☆☆☆☆☆	....	☆☆☆☆☆

MY OVERALL RATING ☆☆☆☆☆

BOOK CLUB NOTES

MY BIGGEST TAKEAWAY

Title: ....

Author: ....

Genre: ....

Format: PAPER / DIGITAL / AUDIO

Recommended by/Why I'm reading it: ....

....

Date started: ....   Date finished: ....

MY ANALYSIS

Would I read it again?   YES / NO

Would I recommend it?   YES / NO
If so, to whom? ....

....

Themes or characters that resonated with me: ....

....

Emotions, thoughts, or memories it brought up in me: ....

....

Opinion about the author or writing style: ....

....

MY RATINGS

WRITING STYLE	☆ ☆ ☆ ☆ ☆	READABILITY	☆ ☆ ☆ ☆ ☆
RELATABILITY	☆ ☆ ☆ ☆ ☆	PERSONAL IMPACT	☆ ☆ ☆ ☆ ☆
ORIGINALITY	☆ ☆ ☆ ☆ ☆	PLOT	☆ ☆ ☆ ☆ ☆
....	☆ ☆ ☆ ☆ ☆	....	☆ ☆ ☆ ☆ ☆
....	☆ ☆ ☆ ☆ ☆	....	☆ ☆ ☆ ☆ ☆
....	☆ ☆ ☆ ☆ ☆	....	☆ ☆ ☆ ☆ ☆

MY OVERALL RATING ☆ ☆ ☆ ☆ ☆

BOOK CLUB NOTES

MY BIGGEST TAKEAWAY

Title: ....

Author: ....

Genre: ....

Format: PAPER / DIGITAL / AUDIO

Recommended by/Why I'm reading it: ....

....

Date started: .... Date finished: ....

MY ANALYSIS

Would I read it again?   YES / NO

Would I recommend it?   YES / NO
If so, to whom? ....

....

Themes or characters that resonated with me: ....

....

Emotions, thoughts, or memories it brought up in me: ....

....

Opinion about the author or writing style: ....

....

MY RATINGS

WRITING STYLE	☆☆☆☆☆	READABILITY	☆☆☆☆☆
RELATABILITY	☆☆☆☆☆	PERSONAL IMPACT	☆☆☆☆☆
ORIGINALITY	☆☆☆☆☆	PLOT	☆☆☆☆☆
....	☆☆☆☆☆	....	☆☆☆☆☆
....	☆☆☆☆☆	....	☆☆☆☆☆
....	☆☆☆☆☆	....	☆☆☆☆☆

MY OVERALL RATING ☆☆☆☆☆

BOOK CLUB NOTES

MY BIGGEST TAKEAWAY

Title: ....

Author: ....

Genre: ....

Format: PAPER / DIGITAL / AUDIO

Recommended by/Why I'm reading it: ....

....

Date started: .... Date finished: ....

MY ANALYSIS

Would I read it again?   YES / NO

Would I recommend it?   YES / NO
If so, to whom? ....

....

Themes or characters that resonated with me: ....

....

Emotions, thoughts, or memories it brought up in me: ......

....

Opinion about the author or writing style: ....

....

MY RATINGS

WRITING STYLE	☆ ☆ ☆ ☆ ☆	READABILITY	☆ ☆ ☆ ☆ ☆
RELATABILITY	☆ ☆ ☆ ☆ ☆	PERSONAL IMPACT	☆ ☆ ☆ ☆ ☆
ORIGINALITY	☆ ☆ ☆ ☆ ☆	PLOT	☆ ☆ ☆ ☆ ☆
....	☆ ☆ ☆ ☆ ☆	....	☆ ☆ ☆ ☆ ☆
....	☆ ☆ ☆ ☆ ☆	....	☆ ☆ ☆ ☆ ☆
....	☆ ☆ ☆ ☆ ☆	....	☆ ☆ ☆ ☆ ☆

MY OVERALL RATING ☆ ☆ ☆ ☆ ☆

BOOK CLUB NOTES

MY BIGGEST TAKEAWAY

Title: ....

Author: ....

Genre: ....

Format: PAPER / DIGITAL / AUDIO

Recommended by/Why I'm reading it: ....

....

Date started: .... Date finished: ....

MY ANALYSIS

Would I read it again?   YES / NO

Would I recommend it?   YES / NO
If so, to whom? ....

....

Themes or characters that resonated with me: ....

....

Emotions, thoughts, or memories it brought up in me: ....

....

Opinion about the author or writing style: ....

....

MY RATINGS

WRITING STYLE	☆ ☆ ☆ ☆ ☆	READABILITY	☆ ☆ ☆ ☆ ☆
RELATABILITY	☆ ☆ ☆ ☆ ☆	PERSONAL IMPACT	☆ ☆ ☆ ☆ ☆
ORIGINALITY	☆ ☆ ☆ ☆ ☆	PLOT	☆ ☆ ☆ ☆ ☆
....	☆ ☆ ☆ ☆ ☆	....	☆ ☆ ☆ ☆ ☆
....	☆ ☆ ☆ ☆ ☆	....	☆ ☆ ☆ ☆ ☆
....	☆ ☆ ☆ ☆ ☆	....	☆ ☆ ☆ ☆ ☆

MY OVERALL RATING   ☆ ☆ ☆ ☆ ☆

BOOK CLUB NOTES

MY BIGGEST TAKEAWAY

Title: ....

Author: ....

Genre: ....

Format: PAPER / DIGITAL / AUDIO

Recommended by/Why I'm reading it: ....

....

Date started: .... Date finished: ....

MY ANALYSIS

Would I read it again?   YES / NO

Would I recommend it?   YES / NO

If so, to whom? ....

....

Themes or characters that resonated with me: ....

....

Emotions, thoughts, or memories it brought up in me: ....

....

Opinion about the author or writing style: ....

....

MY RATINGS

WRITING STYLE	☆☆☆☆☆	READABILITY	☆☆☆☆☆
RELATABILITY	☆☆☆☆☆	PERSONAL IMPACT	☆☆☆☆☆
ORIGINALITY	☆☆☆☆☆	PLOT	☆☆☆☆☆
....	☆☆☆☆☆	....	☆☆☆☆☆
....	☆☆☆☆☆	....	☆☆☆☆☆
....	☆☆☆☆☆	....	☆☆☆☆☆

MY OVERALL RATING ☆☆☆☆☆

BOOK CLUB NOTES

MY BIGGEST TAKEAWAY

Title: ....

Author: ....

Genre: ....

Format: PAPER / DIGITAL / AUDIO

Recommended by/Why I'm reading it: ....

....

Date started: .... Date finished: ....

MY ANALYSIS

Would I read it again?   YES / NO

Would I recommend it?   YES / NO
If so, to whom? ....

....

Themes or characters that resonated with me: ....

....

Emotions, thoughts, or memories it brought up in me: ....

....

Opinion about the author or writing style: ....

....

MY RATINGS

WRITING STYLE	☆ ☆ ☆ ☆ ☆	READABILITY	☆ ☆ ☆ ☆ ☆
RELATABILITY	☆ ☆ ☆ ☆ ☆	PERSONAL IMPACT	☆ ☆ ☆ ☆ ☆
ORIGINALITY	☆ ☆ ☆ ☆ ☆	PLOT	☆ ☆ ☆ ☆ ☆
....	☆ ☆ ☆ ☆ ☆	....	☆ ☆ ☆ ☆ ☆
....	☆ ☆ ☆ ☆ ☆	....	☆ ☆ ☆ ☆ ☆
....	☆ ☆ ☆ ☆ ☆	....	☆ ☆ ☆ ☆ ☆

MY OVERALL RATING   ☆ ☆ ☆ ☆ ☆

BOOK CLUB NOTES

MY BIGGEST TAKEAWAY

Title: ....

Author: ....

Genre: ....

Format: PAPER / DIGITAL / AUDIO

Recommended by/Why I'm reading it: ....

....

Date started: .... Date finished: ....

MY ANALYSIS

Would I read it again?   YES / NO

Would I recommend it?   YES / NO
If so, to whom? ....

....

Themes or characters that resonated with me: ....

....

Emotions, thoughts, or memories it brought up in me: ....

....

Opinion about the author or writing style: ....

....

MY RATINGS

WRITING STYLE	☆☆☆☆☆	READABILITY	☆☆☆☆☆
RELATABILITY	☆☆☆☆☆	PERSONAL IMPACT	☆☆☆☆☆
ORIGINALITY	☆☆☆☆☆	PLOT	☆☆☆☆☆
....	☆☆☆☆☆	....	☆☆☆☆☆
....	☆☆☆☆☆	....	☆☆☆☆☆
....	☆☆☆☆☆	....	☆☆☆☆☆

MY OVERALL RATING ☆☆☆☆☆

BOOK CLUB NOTES

MY BIGGEST TAKEAWAY

Title: ....

Author: ....

Genre: ....

Format: PAPER / DIGITAL / AUDIO

Recommended by/Why I'm reading it: ....
....

Date started: .... Date finished: ....

MY ANALYSIS

Would I read it again?   YES / NO

Would I recommend it?   YES / NO
If so, to whom? ....
....

Themes or characters that resonated with me: ....
....

Emotions, thoughts, or memories it brought up in me: ....
....

Opinion about the author or writing style: ....
....

MY RATINGS

WRITING STYLE	☆☆☆☆☆	READABILITY	☆☆☆☆☆
RELATABILITY	☆☆☆☆☆	PERSONAL IMPACT	☆☆☆☆☆
ORIGINALITY	☆☆☆☆☆	PLOT	☆☆☆☆☆
....	☆☆☆☆☆	....	☆☆☆☆☆
....	☆☆☆☆☆	....	☆☆☆☆☆
....	☆☆☆☆☆	....	☆☆☆☆☆

MY OVERALL RATING ☆☆☆☆☆

BOOK CLUB NOTES

MY BIGGEST TAKEAWAY

Title: ....

Author: ....

Genre: ....

Format: PAPER / DIGITAL / AUDIO

Recommended by/Why I'm reading it: ....
....

Date started: .... Date finished: ....

MY ANALYSIS

Would I read it again?   YES / NO

Would I recommend it?   YES / NO
If so, to whom? ....
....

Themes or characters that resonated with me: ....
....

Emotions, thoughts, or memories it brought up in me: ....
....

Opinion about the author or writing style: ....
....

MY RATINGS

WRITING STYLE	☆ ☆ ☆ ☆ ☆	READABILITY	☆ ☆ ☆ ☆ ☆
RELATABILITY	☆ ☆ ☆ ☆ ☆	PERSONAL IMPACT	☆ ☆ ☆ ☆ ☆
ORIGINALITY	☆ ☆ ☆ ☆ ☆	PLOT	☆ ☆ ☆ ☆ ☆
....	☆ ☆ ☆ ☆ ☆	....	☆ ☆ ☆ ☆ ☆
....	☆ ☆ ☆ ☆ ☆	....	☆ ☆ ☆ ☆ ☆
....	☆ ☆ ☆ ☆ ☆	....	☆ ☆ ☆ ☆ ☆

MY OVERALL RATING ☆ ☆ ☆ ☆ ☆

BOOK CLUB NOTES

....

....

....

....

....

....

....

....

....

....

....

....

....

....

....

....

....

....

....

....

MY BIGGEST TAKEAWAY

....

....

....

....

....

....

Title: ....

Author: ....

Genre: ....

Format: PAPER / DIGITAL / AUDIO

Recommended by/Why I'm reading it: ....

....

Date started: .... Date finished: ....

MY ANALYSIS

Would I read it again?   YES / NO

Would I recommend it?   YES / NO

If so, to whom? ....

....

Themes or characters that resonated with me: ....

....

Emotions, thoughts, or memories it brought up in me: ....

....

Opinion about the author or writing style: ....

....

MY RATINGS

WRITING STYLE	☆☆☆☆☆	READABILITY	☆☆☆☆☆
RELATABILITY	☆☆☆☆☆	PERSONAL IMPACT	☆☆☆☆☆
ORIGINALITY	☆☆☆☆☆	PLOT	☆☆☆☆☆
....	☆☆☆☆☆	....	☆☆☆☆☆
....	☆☆☆☆☆	....	☆☆☆☆☆
....	☆☆☆☆☆	....	☆☆☆☆☆

MY OVERALL RATING ☆☆☆☆☆

BOOK CLUB NOTES

MY BIGGEST TAKEAWAY

Title: ....

Author: ....

Genre: ....

Format: PAPER / DIGITAL / AUDIO

Recommended by/Why I'm reading it: ....

....

Date started: .... Date finished: ....

MY ANALYSIS

Would I read it again?   YES / NO

Would I recommend it?   YES / NO

If so, to whom? ....

....

Themes or characters that resonated with me: ....

....

Emotions, thoughts, or memories it brought up in me: ....

....

Opinion about the author or writing style: ....

....

MY RATINGS

WRITING STYLE	☆☆☆☆☆	READABILITY	☆☆☆☆☆
RELATABILITY	☆☆☆☆☆	PERSONAL IMPACT	☆☆☆☆☆
ORIGINALITY	☆☆☆☆☆	PLOT	☆☆☆☆☆
....	☆☆☆☆☆	....	☆☆☆☆☆
....	☆☆☆☆☆	....	☆☆☆☆☆
....	☆☆☆☆☆	....	☆☆☆☆☆

MY OVERALL RATING ☆☆☆☆☆

BOOK CLUB NOTES

MY BIGGEST TAKEAWAY

Title: ....

Author: ....

Genre: ....

Format: PAPER / DIGITAL / AUDIO

Recommended by/Why I'm reading it: ....

....

Date started: .... Date finished: ....

MY ANALYSIS

Would I read it again?   YES / NO

Would I recommend it?   YES / NO

If so, to whom? ....

....

Themes or characters that resonated with me: ....

....

Emotions, thoughts, or memories it brought up in me: ....

....

Opinion about the author or writing style: ....

....

MY RATINGS

WRITING STYLE	☆ ☆ ☆ ☆ ☆	READABILITY	☆ ☆ ☆ ☆ ☆
RELATABILITY	☆ ☆ ☆ ☆ ☆	PERSONAL IMPACT	☆ ☆ ☆ ☆ ☆
ORIGINALITY	☆ ☆ ☆ ☆ ☆	PLOT	☆ ☆ ☆ ☆ ☆
....	☆ ☆ ☆ ☆ ☆	....	☆ ☆ ☆ ☆ ☆
....	☆ ☆ ☆ ☆ ☆	....	☆ ☆ ☆ ☆ ☆
....	☆ ☆ ☆ ☆ ☆	....	☆ ☆ ☆ ☆ ☆

MY OVERALL RATING ☆ ☆ ☆ ☆ ☆

BOOK CLUB NOTES

MY BIGGEST TAKEAWAY

Title: ....

Author: ....

Genre: ....

Format: PAPER / DIGITAL / AUDIO

Recommended by/Why I'm reading it: ....

....

Date started: .... Date finished: ....

MY ANALYSIS

Would I read it again?   YES / NO

Would I recommend it?   YES / NO

If so, to whom? ....

....

Themes or characters that resonated with me: ....

....

Emotions, thoughts, or memories it brought up in me: ....

....

Opinion about the author or writing style: ....

....

MY RATINGS

WRITING STYLE	☆☆☆☆☆	READABILITY	☆☆☆☆☆
RELATABILITY	☆☆☆☆☆	PERSONAL IMPACT	☆☆☆☆☆
ORIGINALITY	☆☆☆☆☆	PLOT	☆☆☆☆☆
....	☆☆☆☆☆	....	☆☆☆☆☆
....	☆☆☆☆☆	....	☆☆☆☆☆
....	☆☆☆☆☆	....	☆☆☆☆☆

MY OVERALL RATING ☆☆☆☆☆

BOOK CLUB NOTES

MY BIGGEST TAKEAWAY

Title: ....

Author: ....

Genre: ....

Format: PAPER / DIGITAL / AUDIO

Recommended by/Why I'm reading it: ....

....

Date started: .... Date finished: ....

MY ANALYSIS

Would I read it again?   YES / NO

Would I recommend it?   YES / NO
If so, to whom? ....

....

Themes or characters that resonated with me: ....

....

Emotions, thoughts, or memories it brought up in me: ....

....

Opinion about the author or writing style: ....

....

MY RATINGS

WRITING STYLE	☆☆☆☆☆	READABILITY	☆☆☆☆☆
RELATABILITY	☆☆☆☆☆	PERSONAL IMPACT	☆☆☆☆☆
ORIGINALITY	☆☆☆☆☆	PLOT	☆☆☆☆☆
....	☆☆☆☆☆	....	☆☆☆☆☆
....	☆☆☆☆☆	....	☆☆☆☆☆
....	☆☆☆☆☆	....	☆☆☆☆☆

MY OVERALL RATING ☆☆☆☆☆

BOOK CLUB NOTES

MY BIGGEST TAKEAWAY

Title: ....

Author: ....

Genre: ....

Format: PAPER / DIGITAL / AUDIO

Recommended by/Why I'm reading it: ....
....

Date started: .... Date finished: ....

MY ANALYSIS

Would I read it again?   YES / NO

Would I recommend it?   YES / NO
If so, to whom? ....
....

Themes or characters that resonated with me: ....
....

Emotions, thoughts, or memories it brought up in me: .....
....

Opinion about the author or writing style: ....
....

MY RATINGS

WRITING STYLE	☆☆☆☆☆	READABILITY	☆☆☆☆☆
RELATABILITY	☆☆☆☆☆	PERSONAL IMPACT	☆☆☆☆☆
ORIGINALITY	☆☆☆☆☆	PLOT	☆☆☆☆☆
....	☆☆☆☆☆	....	☆☆☆☆☆
....	☆☆☆☆☆	....	☆☆☆☆☆
....	☆☆☆☆☆	....	☆☆☆☆☆

MY OVERALL RATING ☆☆☆☆☆

BOOK CLUB NOTES

MY BIGGEST TAKEAWAY

Title: ....

Author: ....

Genre: ....

Format: PAPER / DIGITAL / AUDIO

Recommended by/Why I'm reading it: ....

....

Date started: .... Date finished: ....

MY ANALYSIS

Would I read it again?   YES / NO

Would I recommend it?   YES / NO
If so, to whom? ....

....

Themes or characters that resonated with me: ....

....

Emotions, thoughts, or memories it brought up in me: ....

....

Opinion about the author or writing style: ....

....

MY RATINGS

WRITING STYLE	☆ ☆ ☆ ☆ ☆	READABILITY	☆ ☆ ☆ ☆ ☆
RELATABILITY	☆ ☆ ☆ ☆ ☆	PERSONAL IMPACT	☆ ☆ ☆ ☆ ☆
ORIGINALITY	☆ ☆ ☆ ☆ ☆	PLOT	☆ ☆ ☆ ☆ ☆
....	☆ ☆ ☆ ☆ ☆	....	☆ ☆ ☆ ☆ ☆
....	☆ ☆ ☆ ☆ ☆	....	☆ ☆ ☆ ☆ ☆
....	☆ ☆ ☆ ☆ ☆	....	☆ ☆ ☆ ☆ ☆

MY OVERALL RATING ☆ ☆ ☆ ☆ ☆

BOOK CLUB NOTES

MY BIGGEST TAKEAWAY

Title: ....

Author: ....

Genre: ....

Format: PAPER / DIGITAL / AUDIO

Recommended by/Why I'm reading it: ....

....

Date started: .... Date finished: ....

MY ANALYSIS

Would I read it again? YES / NO

Would I recommend it? YES / NO

If so, to whom? ....

....

Themes or characters that resonated with me: ....

....

Emotions, thoughts, or memories it brought up in me: ....

....

Opinion about the author or writing style: ....

....

MY RATINGS

WRITING STYLE	☆ ☆ ☆ ☆ ☆	READABILITY	☆ ☆ ☆ ☆ ☆
RELATABILITY	☆ ☆ ☆ ☆ ☆	PERSONAL IMPACT	☆ ☆ ☆ ☆ ☆
ORIGINALITY	☆ ☆ ☆ ☆ ☆	PLOT	☆ ☆ ☆ ☆ ☆
....	☆ ☆ ☆ ☆ ☆	....	☆ ☆ ☆ ☆ ☆
....	☆ ☆ ☆ ☆ ☆	....	☆ ☆ ☆ ☆ ☆
....	☆ ☆ ☆ ☆ ☆	....	☆ ☆ ☆ ☆ ☆

MY OVERALL RATING ☆ ☆ ☆ ☆ ☆

BOOK CLUB NOTES

MY BIGGEST TAKEAWAY

Title: ....

Author: ....

Genre: ....

Format: PAPER / DIGITAL / AUDIO

Recommended by/Why I'm reading it: ....

....

Date started: .... Date finished: ....

MY ANALYSIS

Would I read it again?   YES / NO

Would I recommend it?   YES / NO

If so, to whom? ....

....

Themes or characters that resonated with me: ....

....

Emotions, thoughts, or memories it brought up in me: ....

....

Opinion about the author or writing style: ....

....

MY RATINGS

WRITING STYLE	☆☆☆☆☆	READABILITY	☆☆☆☆☆
RELATABILITY	☆☆☆☆☆	PERSONAL IMPACT	☆☆☆☆☆
ORIGINALITY	☆☆☆☆☆	PLOT	☆☆☆☆☆
....	☆☆☆☆☆	....	☆☆☆☆☆
....	☆☆☆☆☆	....	☆☆☆☆☆
....	☆☆☆☆☆	....	☆☆☆☆☆

MY OVERALL RATING ☆☆☆☆☆

BOOK CLUB NOTES

MY BIGGEST TAKEAWAY

Title: ....

Author: ....

Genre: ....

Format: PAPER / DIGITAL / AUDIO

Recommended by/Why I'm reading it: ....

....

Date started: .... Date finished: ....

MY ANALYSIS

Would I read it again?   YES / NO

Would I recommend it?   YES / NO

If so, to whom? ....

....

Themes or characters that resonated with me: ....

....

Emotions, thoughts, or memories it brought up in me: ....

....

Opinion about the author or writing style: ....

....

MY RATINGS

WRITING STYLE	☆ ☆ ☆ ☆ ☆	READABILITY	☆ ☆ ☆ ☆ ☆
RELATABILITY	☆ ☆ ☆ ☆ ☆	PERSONAL IMPACT	☆ ☆ ☆ ☆ ☆
ORIGINALITY	☆ ☆ ☆ ☆ ☆	PLOT	☆ ☆ ☆ ☆ ☆
....	☆ ☆ ☆ ☆ ☆	....	☆ ☆ ☆ ☆ ☆
....	☆ ☆ ☆ ☆ ☆	....	☆ ☆ ☆ ☆ ☆
....	☆ ☆ ☆ ☆ ☆	....	☆ ☆ ☆ ☆ ☆

MY OVERALL RATING ☆ ☆ ☆ ☆ ☆

BOOK CLUB NOTES

MY BIGGEST TAKEAWAY

Title: ....

Author: ....

Genre: ....

Format: PAPER / DIGITAL / AUDIO

Recommended by/Why I'm reading it: ....

....

Date started: .... Date finished: ....

MY ANALYSIS

Would I read it again?   YES / NO

Would I recommend it?   YES / NO

If so, to whom? ....

Themes or characters that resonated with me: ....

Emotions, thoughts, or memories it brought up in me: ....

Opinion about the author or writing style: ....

....

MY RATINGS

WRITING STYLE	☆ ☆ ☆ ☆ ☆	READABILITY	☆ ☆ ☆ ☆ ☆
RELATABILITY	☆ ☆ ☆ ☆ ☆	PERSONAL IMPACT	☆ ☆ ☆ ☆ ☆
ORIGINALITY	☆ ☆ ☆ ☆ ☆	PLOT	☆ ☆ ☆ ☆ ☆
....	☆ ☆ ☆ ☆ ☆	....	☆ ☆ ☆ ☆ ☆
....	☆ ☆ ☆ ☆ ☆	....	☆ ☆ ☆ ☆ ☆
....	☆ ☆ ☆ ☆ ☆	....	☆ ☆ ☆ ☆ ☆

MY OVERALL RATING ☆ ☆ ☆ ☆ ☆

BOOK CLUB NOTES

MY BIGGEST TAKEAWAY

Title: ....

Author: ....

Genre: ....

Format: PAPER / DIGITAL / AUDIO

Recommended by/Why I'm reading it: ....
....

Date started: .... Date finished: ....

MY ANALYSIS

Would I read it again?   YES / NO

Would I recommend it?   YES / NO
If so, to whom? ....
....

Themes or characters that resonated with me: ....
....

Emotions, thoughts, or memories it brought up in me: ....
....

Opinion about the author or writing style: ....
....

MY RATINGS

WRITING STYLE	☆ ☆ ☆ ☆ ☆	READABILITY	☆ ☆ ☆ ☆ ☆
RELATABILITY	☆ ☆ ☆ ☆ ☆	PERSONAL IMPACT	☆ ☆ ☆ ☆ ☆
ORIGINALITY	☆ ☆ ☆ ☆ ☆	PLOT	☆ ☆ ☆ ☆ ☆
....	☆ ☆ ☆ ☆ ☆	....	☆ ☆ ☆ ☆ ☆
....	☆ ☆ ☆ ☆ ☆	....	☆ ☆ ☆ ☆ ☆
....	☆ ☆ ☆ ☆ ☆	....	☆ ☆ ☆ ☆ ☆

MY OVERALL RATING ☆ ☆ ☆ ☆ ☆

BOOK CLUB NOTES

MY BIGGEST TAKEAWAY

Title: ....

Author: ....

Genre: ....

Format: PAPER / DIGITAL / AUDIO

Recommended by/Why I'm reading it: ....

....

Date started: .... Date finished: ....

MY ANALYSIS

Would I read it again?   YES / NO

Would I recommend it?   YES / NO
If so, to whom? ....

....

Themes or characters that resonated with me: ....

....

Emotions, thoughts, or memories it brought up in me: ......

....

Opinion about the author or writing style: ....

....

MY RATINGS

WRITING STYLE	☆☆☆☆☆	READABILITY	☆☆☆☆☆
RELATABILITY	☆☆☆☆☆	PERSONAL IMPACT	☆☆☆☆☆
ORIGINALITY	☆☆☆☆☆	PLOT	☆☆☆☆☆
....	☆☆☆☆☆	....	☆☆☆☆☆
....	☆☆☆☆☆	....	☆☆☆☆☆
....	☆☆☆☆☆	....	☆☆☆☆☆

MY OVERALL RATING ☆☆☆☆☆

BOOK CLUB NOTES

MY BIGGEST TAKEAWAY

Title: ....

Author: ....

Genre: ....

Format: PAPER / DIGITAL / AUDIO

Recommended by/Why I'm reading it: ....

....

Date started: ....   Date finished: ....

MY ANALYSIS

Would I read it again?   YES / NO

Would I recommend it?   YES / NO

If so, to whom? ....

....

Themes or characters that resonated with me: ....

....

Emotions, thoughts, or memories it brought up in me: ....

....

Opinion about the author or writing style: ....

....

MY RATINGS

WRITING STYLE	☆☆☆☆☆	READABILITY	☆☆☆☆☆
RELATABILITY	☆☆☆☆☆	PERSONAL IMPACT	☆☆☆☆☆
ORIGINALITY	☆☆☆☆☆	PLOT	☆☆☆☆☆
....	☆☆☆☆☆	....	☆☆☆☆☆
....	☆☆☆☆☆	....	☆☆☆☆☆
....	☆☆☆☆☆	....	☆☆☆☆☆

MY OVERALL RATING ☆☆☆☆☆

BOOK CLUB NOTES

MY BIGGEST TAKEAWAY

Title: ....

Author: ....

Genre: ....

Format: PAPER / DIGITAL / AUDIO

Recommended by/Why I'm reading it: ....

....

Date started: .... Date finished: ....

MY ANALYSIS

Would I read it again?   YES / NO

Would I recommend it?   YES / NO

If so, to whom? ....

....

Themes or characters that resonated with me: ....

....

Emotions, thoughts, or memories it brought up in me: ....

....

Opinion about the author or writing style: ....

....

MY RATINGS

WRITING STYLE	☆ ☆ ☆ ☆ ☆	READABILITY	☆ ☆ ☆ ☆ ☆
RELATABILITY	☆ ☆ ☆ ☆ ☆	PERSONAL IMPACT	☆ ☆ ☆ ☆ ☆
ORIGINALITY	☆ ☆ ☆ ☆ ☆	PLOT	☆ ☆ ☆ ☆ ☆
....	☆ ☆ ☆ ☆ ☆	....	☆ ☆ ☆ ☆ ☆
....	☆ ☆ ☆ ☆ ☆	....	☆ ☆ ☆ ☆ ☆
....	☆ ☆ ☆ ☆ ☆	....	☆ ☆ ☆ ☆ ☆

MY OVERALL RATING ☆ ☆ ☆ ☆ ☆

BOOK CLUB NOTES

MY BIGGEST TAKEAWAY

Title: ....

Author: ....

Genre: ....

Format: PAPER / DIGITAL / AUDIO

Recommended by/Why I'm reading it: ....

....

Date started: ....   Date finished: ....

MY ANALYSIS

Would I read it again?   YES / NO

Would I recommend it?   YES / NO
If so, to whom? ....

....

Themes or characters that resonated with me: ....

....

Emotions, thoughts, or memories it brought up in me: ....

....

Opinion about the author or writing style: ....

....

MY RATINGS

WRITING STYLE	☆☆☆☆☆	READABILITY	☆☆☆☆☆
RELATABILITY	☆☆☆☆☆	PERSONAL IMPACT	☆☆☆☆☆
ORIGINALITY	☆☆☆☆☆	PLOT	☆☆☆☆☆
....	☆☆☆☆☆	....	☆☆☆☆☆
....	☆☆☆☆☆	....	☆☆☆☆☆
....	☆☆☆☆☆	....	☆☆☆☆☆

MY OVERALL RATING ☆☆☆☆☆

BOOK CLUB NOTES

MY BIGGEST TAKEAWAY

Title: ....

Author: ....

Genre: ....

Format: PAPER / DIGITAL / AUDIO

Recommended by/Why I'm reading it: ....

....

Date started: .... Date finished: ....

MY ANALYSIS

Would I read it again?   YES / NO

Would I recommend it?   YES / NO

If so, to whom? ....

....

Themes or characters that resonated with me: ....

....

Emotions, thoughts, or memories it brought up in me: ....

....

Opinion about the author or writing style: ....

....

MY RATINGS

WRITING STYLE	☆☆☆☆☆	READABILITY	☆☆☆☆☆
RELATABILITY	☆☆☆☆☆	PERSONAL IMPACT	☆☆☆☆☆
ORIGINALITY	☆☆☆☆☆	PLOT	☆☆☆☆☆
....	☆☆☆☆☆	....	☆☆☆☆☆
....	☆☆☆☆☆	....	☆☆☆☆☆
....	☆☆☆☆☆	....	☆☆☆☆☆

MY OVERALL RATING ☆☆☆☆☆

BOOK CLUB NOTES

MY BIGGEST TAKEAWAY

Title: ....

Author: ....

Genre: ....

Format: PAPER / DIGITAL / AUDIO

Recommended by/Why I'm reading it: ....

....

Date started: .... Date finished: ....

MY ANALYSIS

Would I read it again?   YES / NO

Would I recommend it?   YES / NO

If so, to whom? ....

....

Themes or characters that resonated with me: ....

....

Emotions, thoughts, or memories it brought up in me: ....

....

Opinion about the author or writing style: ....

....

MY RATINGS

WRITING STYLE	☆ ☆ ☆ ☆ ☆	READABILITY	☆ ☆ ☆ ☆ ☆
RELATABILITY	☆ ☆ ☆ ☆ ☆	PERSONAL IMPACT	☆ ☆ ☆ ☆ ☆
ORIGINALITY	☆ ☆ ☆ ☆ ☆	PLOT	☆ ☆ ☆ ☆ ☆
....	☆ ☆ ☆ ☆ ☆	....	☆ ☆ ☆ ☆ ☆
....	☆ ☆ ☆ ☆ ☆	....	☆ ☆ ☆ ☆ ☆
....	☆ ☆ ☆ ☆ ☆	....	☆ ☆ ☆ ☆ ☆

MY OVERALL RATING ☆ ☆ ☆ ☆ ☆

BOOK CLUB NOTES

MY BIGGEST TAKEAWAY

Title: ....

Author: ....

Genre: ....

Format: PAPER / DIGITAL / AUDIO

Recommended by/Why I'm reading it: ....

....

Date started: .... Date finished: ....

MY ANALYSIS

Would I read it again?   YES / NO

Would I recommend it?   YES / NO

If so, to whom? ....

....

Themes or characters that resonated with me: ....

....

Emotions, thoughts, or memories it brought up in me: ....

....

Opinion about the author or writing style: ....

....

MY RATINGS

WRITING STYLE	☆ ☆ ☆ ☆ ☆	READABILITY	☆ ☆ ☆ ☆ ☆
RELATABILITY	☆ ☆ ☆ ☆ ☆	PERSONAL IMPACT	☆ ☆ ☆ ☆ ☆
ORIGINALITY	☆ ☆ ☆ ☆ ☆	PLOT	☆ ☆ ☆ ☆ ☆
....	☆ ☆ ☆ ☆ ☆	....	☆ ☆ ☆ ☆ ☆
....	☆ ☆ ☆ ☆ ☆	....	☆ ☆ ☆ ☆ ☆
....	☆ ☆ ☆ ☆ ☆	....	☆ ☆ ☆ ☆ ☆

MY OVERALL RATING ☆ ☆ ☆ ☆ ☆

BOOK CLUB NOTES

MY BIGGEST TAKEAWAY

Title: ....

Author: ....

Genre: ....

Format: PAPER / DIGITAL / AUDIO

Recommended by/Why I'm reading it: ....

....

Date started: .... Date finished: ....

MY ANALYSIS

Would I read it again?   YES / NO

Would I recommend it?   YES / NO

If so, to whom? ....

....

Themes or characters that resonated with me: ....

....

Emotions, thoughts, or memories it brought up in me: ....

....

Opinion about the author or writing style: ....

....

MY RATINGS

WRITING STYLE	☆☆☆☆☆	READABILITY	☆☆☆☆☆
RELATABILITY	☆☆☆☆☆	PERSONAL IMPACT	☆☆☆☆☆
ORIGINALITY	☆☆☆☆☆	PLOT	☆☆☆☆☆
....	☆☆☆☆☆	....	☆☆☆☆☆
....	☆☆☆☆☆	....	☆☆☆☆☆
....	☆☆☆☆☆	....	☆☆☆☆☆

MY OVERALL RATING ☆☆☆☆☆

BOOK CLUB NOTES

MY BIGGEST TAKEAWAY

Title: ....

Author: ....

Genre: ....

Format: PAPER / DIGITAL / AUDIO

Recommended by/Why I'm reading it: ....

....

Date started: .... Date finished: ....

MY ANALYSIS

Would I read it again?   YES / NO

Would I recommend it?   YES / NO
If so, to whom? ....

....

Themes or characters that resonated with me: ....

....

Emotions, thoughts, or memories it brought up in me: ....

....

Opinion about the author or writing style: ....

....

MY RATINGS

WRITING STYLE	☆ ☆ ☆ ☆ ☆	READABILITY	☆ ☆ ☆ ☆ ☆
RELATABILITY	☆ ☆ ☆ ☆ ☆	PERSONAL IMPACT	☆ ☆ ☆ ☆ ☆
ORIGINALITY	☆ ☆ ☆ ☆ ☆	PLOT	☆ ☆ ☆ ☆ ☆
....	☆ ☆ ☆ ☆ ☆	....	☆ ☆ ☆ ☆ ☆
....	☆ ☆ ☆ ☆ ☆	....	☆ ☆ ☆ ☆ ☆
....	☆ ☆ ☆ ☆ ☆	....	☆ ☆ ☆ ☆ ☆

MY OVERALL RATING ☆ ☆ ☆ ☆ ☆

BOOK CLUB NOTES

MY BIGGEST TAKEAWAY

Title: ....

Author: ....

Genre: ....

Format: PAPER / DIGITAL / AUDIO

Recommended by/Why I'm reading it: ....

....

Date started: .... Date finished: ....

MY ANALYSIS

Would I read it again?   YES / NO

Would I recommend it?   YES / NO
If so, to whom? ....

....

Themes or characters that resonated with me: ....

....

Emotions, thoughts, or memories it brought up in me: ....

....

Opinion about the author or writing style: ....

....

MY RATINGS

WRITING STYLE	☆☆☆☆☆	READABILITY	☆☆☆☆☆
RELATABILITY	☆☆☆☆☆	PERSONAL IMPACT	☆☆☆☆☆
ORIGINALITY	☆☆☆☆☆	PLOT	☆☆☆☆☆
....	☆☆☆☆☆	....	☆☆☆☆☆
....	☆☆☆☆☆	....	☆☆☆☆☆
....	☆☆☆☆☆	....	☆☆☆☆☆

MY OVERALL RATING ☆☆☆☆☆

BOOK CLUB NOTES

MY BIGGEST TAKEAWAY

Title: ....

Author: ....

Genre: ....

Format: PAPER / DIGITAL / AUDIO

Recommended by/Why I'm reading it: ....

....

Date started: .... Date finished: ....

MY ANALYSIS

Would I read it again?   YES / NO

Would I recommend it?   YES / NO
If so, to whom? ....

....

Themes or characters that resonated with me: ....

....

Emotions, thoughts, or memories it brought up in me: ....

....

Opinion about the author or writing style: ....

....

MY RATINGS

WRITING STYLE	☆☆☆☆☆	READABILITY	☆☆☆☆☆
RELATABILITY	☆☆☆☆☆	PERSONAL IMPACT	☆☆☆☆☆
ORIGINALITY	☆☆☆☆☆	PLOT	☆☆☆☆☆
....	☆☆☆☆☆	....	☆☆☆☆☆
....	☆☆☆☆☆	....	☆☆☆☆☆
....	☆☆☆☆☆	....	☆☆☆☆☆

MY OVERALL RATING ☆☆☆☆☆

BOOK CLUB NOTES

MY BIGGEST TAKEAWAY

Title: ....

Author: ....

Genre: ....

Format: PAPER / DIGITAL / AUDIO

Recommended by/Why I'm reading it: ....

....

Date started: ....   Date finished: ....

MY ANALYSIS

Would I read it again?   YES / NO

Would I recommend it?   YES / NO
If so, to whom? ....

....

Themes or characters that resonated with me: ....

....

Emotions, thoughts, or memories it brought up in me: ....

....

Opinion about the author or writing style: ....

....

MY RATINGS

WRITING STYLE	☆☆☆☆☆	READABILITY	☆☆☆☆☆
RELATABILITY	☆☆☆☆☆	PERSONAL IMPACT	☆☆☆☆☆
ORIGINALITY	☆☆☆☆☆	PLOT	☆☆☆☆☆
....	☆☆☆☆☆	....	☆☆☆☆☆
....	☆☆☆☆☆	....	☆☆☆☆☆
....	☆☆☆☆☆	....	☆☆☆☆☆

MY OVERALL RATING ☆☆☆☆☆

BOOK CLUB NOTES

MY BIGGEST TAKEAWAY

Title: ....

Author: ....

Genre: ....

Format: PAPER / DIGITAL / AUDIO

Recommended by/Why I'm reading it: ....

....

Date started: .... Date finished: ....

MY ANALYSIS

Would I read it again?　YES / NO

Would I recommend it?　YES / NO

If so, to whom? ....

....

Themes or characters that resonated with me: ....

....

Emotions, thoughts, or memories it brought up in me: ....

....

Opinion about the author or writing style: ....

....

MY RATINGS

WRITING STYLE	☆☆☆☆☆	READABILITY	☆☆☆☆☆
RELATABILITY	☆☆☆☆☆	PERSONAL IMPACT	☆☆☆☆☆
ORIGINALITY	☆☆☆☆☆	PLOT	☆☆☆☆☆
....	☆☆☆☆☆	....	☆☆☆☆☆
....	☆☆☆☆☆	....	☆☆☆☆☆
....	☆☆☆☆☆	....	☆☆☆☆☆

MY OVERALL RATING ☆☆☆☆☆

BOOK CLUB NOTES

MY BIGGEST TAKEAWAY

Title: ....

Author: ....

Genre: ....

Format: PAPER / DIGITAL / AUDIO

Recommended by/Why I'm reading it: ....

....

Date started: .... Date finished: ....

MY ANALYSIS

Would I read it again?   YES / NO

Would I recommend it?   YES / NO
If so, to whom? ....

....

Themes or characters that resonated with me: ....

....

Emotions, thoughts, or memories it brought up in me: ....

....

Opinion about the author or writing style: ....

....

MY RATINGS

WRITING STYLE	☆ ☆ ☆ ☆ ☆	READABILITY	☆ ☆ ☆ ☆ ☆
RELATABILITY	☆ ☆ ☆ ☆ ☆	PERSONAL IMPACT	☆ ☆ ☆ ☆ ☆
ORIGINALITY	☆ ☆ ☆ ☆ ☆	PLOT	☆ ☆ ☆ ☆ ☆
....	☆ ☆ ☆ ☆ ☆	....	☆ ☆ ☆ ☆ ☆
....	☆ ☆ ☆ ☆ ☆	....	☆ ☆ ☆ ☆ ☆
....	☆ ☆ ☆ ☆ ☆	....	☆ ☆ ☆ ☆ ☆

MY OVERALL RATING ☆ ☆ ☆ ☆ ☆

BOOK CLUB NOTES

MY BIGGEST TAKEAWAY

Title: ....

Author: ....

Genre: ....

Format: PAPER / DIGITAL / AUDIO

Recommended by/Why I'm reading it: ....

....

Date started: .... Date finished: ....

MY ANALYSIS

Would I read it again?   YES / NO

Would I recommend it?   YES / NO
If so, to whom? ....

....

Themes or characters that resonated with me: ....

....

Emotions, thoughts, or memories it brought up in me: ....

....

Opinion about the author or writing style: ....

....

MY RATINGS

WRITING STYLE	☆☆☆☆☆	READABILITY	☆☆☆☆☆
RELATABILITY	☆☆☆☆☆	PERSONAL IMPACT	☆☆☆☆☆
ORIGINALITY	☆☆☆☆☆	PLOT	☆☆☆☆☆
....	☆☆☆☆☆	....	☆☆☆☆☆
....	☆☆☆☆☆	....	☆☆☆☆☆
....	☆☆☆☆☆	....	☆☆☆☆☆

MY OVERALL RATING ☆☆☆☆☆

BOOK CLUB NOTES

MY BIGGEST TAKEAWAY

Title: ....

Author: ....

Genre: ....

Format: PAPER / DIGITAL / AUDIO

Recommended by/Why I'm reading it: ....
....

Date started: ....   Date finished: ....

MY ANALYSIS

Would I read it again?   YES / NO

Would I recommend it?   YES / NO
If so, to whom? ....
....

Themes or characters that resonated with me: ....
....

Emotions, thoughts, or memories it brought up in me: ....
....

Opinion about the author or writing style: ....
....

MY RATINGS

WRITING STYLE	☆☆☆☆☆	READABILITY	☆☆☆☆☆
RELATABILITY	☆☆☆☆☆	PERSONAL IMPACT	☆☆☆☆☆
ORIGINALITY	☆☆☆☆☆	PLOT	☆☆☆☆☆
....	☆☆☆☆☆	....	☆☆☆☆☆
....	☆☆☆☆☆	....	☆☆☆☆☆
....	☆☆☆☆☆	....	☆☆☆☆☆

MY OVERALL RATING ☆☆☆☆☆

BOOK CLUB NOTES

MY BIGGEST TAKEAWAY

Title: ....

Author: ....

Genre: ....

Format: PAPER / DIGITAL / AUDIO

Recommended by/Why I'm reading it: ....

....

Date started: ....   Date finished: ....

MY ANALYSIS

Would I read it again?   YES / NO

Would I recommend it?   YES / NO
If so, to whom? ....

....

Themes or characters that resonated with me: ....

....

Emotions, thoughts, or memories it brought up in me: ....

....

Opinion about the author or writing style: ....

....

MY RATINGS

WRITING STYLE	☆☆☆☆☆	READABILITY	☆☆☆☆☆
RELATABILITY	☆☆☆☆☆	PERSONAL IMPACT	☆☆☆☆☆
ORIGINALITY	☆☆☆☆☆	PLOT	☆☆☆☆☆
....	☆☆☆☆☆	....	☆☆☆☆☆
....	☆☆☆☆☆	....	☆☆☆☆☆
....	☆☆☆☆☆	....	☆☆☆☆☆

MY OVERALL RATING ☆☆☆☆☆

BOOK CLUB NOTES

MY BIGGEST TAKEAWAY

Title: ....

Author: ....

Genre: ....

Format: PAPER / DIGITAL / AUDIO

Recommended by/Why I'm reading it: ....

....

Date started: .... Date finished: ....

MY ANALYSIS

Would I read it again?   YES / NO

Would I recommend it?   YES / NO
If so, to whom? ....

....

Themes or characters that resonated with me: ....

....

Emotions, thoughts, or memories it brought up in me: .....

....

Opinion about the author or writing style: ....

....

MY RATINGS

WRITING STYLE	☆ ☆ ☆ ☆ ☆	READABILITY	☆ ☆ ☆ ☆ ☆
RELATABILITY	☆ ☆ ☆ ☆ ☆	PERSONAL IMPACT	☆ ☆ ☆ ☆ ☆
ORIGINALITY	☆ ☆ ☆ ☆ ☆	PLOT	☆ ☆ ☆ ☆ ☆
....	☆ ☆ ☆ ☆ ☆	....	☆ ☆ ☆ ☆ ☆
....	☆ ☆ ☆ ☆ ☆	....	☆ ☆ ☆ ☆ ☆
....	☆ ☆ ☆ ☆ ☆	....	☆ ☆ ☆ ☆ ☆

MY OVERALL RATING ☆ ☆ ☆ ☆ ☆

BOOK CLUB NOTES

MY BIGGEST TAKEAWAY

Title: ....

Author: ....

Genre: ....

Format: PAPER / DIGITAL / AUDIO

Recommended by/Why I'm reading it: ....
....

Date started: .... Date finished: ....

MY ANALYSIS

Would I read it again?   YES / NO

Would I recommend it?   YES / NO
If so, to whom? ....
....

Themes or characters that resonated with me: ....
....

Emotions, thoughts, or memories it brought up in me: ....
....

Opinion about the author or writing style: ....
....

MY RATINGS

WRITING STYLE	☆☆☆☆☆	READABILITY	☆☆☆☆☆
RELATABILITY	☆☆☆☆☆	PERSONAL IMPACT	☆☆☆☆☆
ORIGINALITY	☆☆☆☆☆	PLOT	☆☆☆☆☆
....	☆☆☆☆☆	....	☆☆☆☆☆
....	☆☆☆☆☆	....	☆☆☆☆☆
....	☆☆☆☆☆	....	☆☆☆☆☆

MY OVERALL RATING ☆☆☆☆☆

BOOK CLUB NOTES

MY BIGGEST TAKEAWAY

Title: ....

Author: ....

Genre: ....

Format: PAPER / DIGITAL / AUDIO

Recommended by/Why I'm reading it: ....

....

Date started: .... Date finished: ....

MY ANALYSIS

Would I read it again?   YES / NO

Would I recommend it?   YES / NO
If so, to whom? ....

....

Themes or characters that resonated with me: ....

....

Emotions, thoughts, or memories it brought up in me: ....

....

Opinion about the author or writing style: ....

....

MY RATINGS

WRITING STYLE	☆☆☆☆☆	READABILITY	☆☆☆☆☆
RELATABILITY	☆☆☆☆☆	PERSONAL IMPACT	☆☆☆☆☆
ORIGINALITY	☆☆☆☆☆	PLOT	☆☆☆☆☆
....	☆☆☆☆☆	....	☆☆☆☆☆
....	☆☆☆☆☆	....	☆☆☆☆☆
....	☆☆☆☆☆	....	☆☆☆☆☆

MY OVERALL RATING ☆☆☆☆☆

BOOK CLUB NOTES

MY BIGGEST TAKEAWAY

Title: ....

Author: ....

Genre: ....

Format: PAPER / DIGITAL / AUDIO

Recommended by/Why I'm reading it: ....

....

Date started: .... Date finished: ....

MY ANALYSIS

Would I read it again?   YES / NO

Would I recommend it?   YES / NO

If so, to whom? ....

....

Themes or characters that resonated with me: ....

....

Emotions, thoughts, or memories it brought up in me: ....

....

Opinion about the author or writing style: ....

....

MY RATINGS

WRITING STYLE	☆☆☆☆☆	READABILITY	☆☆☆☆☆
RELATABILITY	☆☆☆☆☆	PERSONAL IMPACT	☆☆☆☆☆
ORIGINALITY	☆☆☆☆☆	PLOT	☆☆☆☆☆
....	☆☆☆☆☆	....	☆☆☆☆☆
....	☆☆☆☆☆	....	☆☆☆☆☆
....	☆☆☆☆☆	....	☆☆☆☆☆

MY OVERALL RATING ☆☆☆☆☆

BOOK CLUB NOTES

_____

_____

_____

_____

_____

_____

_____

_____

_____

_____

_____

_____

_____

_____

_____

_____

_____

_____

MY BIGGEST TAKEAWAY

_____

_____

_____

_____

_____

_____

Title: ....

Author: ....

Genre: ....

Format: PAPER / DIGITAL / AUDIO

Recommended by/Why I'm reading it: ....

....

Date started: .... Date finished: ....

MY ANALYSIS

Would I read it again?   YES / NO

Would I recommend it?   YES / NO

If so, to whom? ....

....

Themes or characters that resonated with me: ....

....

Emotions, thoughts, or memories it brought up in me: ....

....

Opinion about the author or writing style: ....

....

MY RATINGS

WRITING STYLE	☆☆☆☆☆	READABILITY	☆☆☆☆☆
RELATABILITY	☆☆☆☆☆	PERSONAL IMPACT	☆☆☆☆☆
ORIGINALITY	☆☆☆☆☆	PLOT	☆☆☆☆☆
....	☆☆☆☆☆	....	☆☆☆☆☆
....	☆☆☆☆☆	....	☆☆☆☆☆
....	☆☆☆☆☆	....	☆☆☆☆☆

MY OVERALL RATING ☆☆☆☆☆

BOOK CLUB NOTES

MY BIGGEST TAKEAWAY

Title: ....

Author: ....

Genre: ....

Format: PAPER / DIGITAL / AUDIO

Recommended by/Why I'm reading it: ....

....

Date started: .... Date finished: ....

MY ANALYSIS

Would I read it again?   YES / NO

Would I recommend it?   YES / NO

If so, to whom? ....

....

Themes or characters that resonated with me: ....

....

Emotions, thoughts, or memories it brought up in me: ....

....

Opinion about the author or writing style: ....

....

MY RATINGS

WRITING STYLE	☆☆☆☆☆	READABILITY ☆☆☆☆☆
RELATABILITY	☆☆☆☆☆	PERSONAL IMPACT ☆☆☆☆☆
ORIGINALITY	☆☆☆☆☆	PLOT ☆☆☆☆☆
....	☆☆☆☆☆	.... ☆☆☆☆☆
....	☆☆☆☆☆	.... ☆☆☆☆☆
....	☆☆☆☆☆	.... ☆☆☆☆☆

MY OVERALL RATING ☆☆☆☆☆

BOOK CLUB NOTES

_____
_____
_____
_____
_____
_____
_____
_____
_____
_____
_____
_____
_____
_____
_____
_____
_____
_____
_____
_____

MY BIGGEST TAKEAWAY

_____
_____
_____
_____
_____
_____

Title: ....

Author: ....

Genre: ....

Format: PAPER / DIGITAL / AUDIO

Recommended by/Why I'm reading it: ....

....

Date started: .... Date finished: ....

MY ANALYSIS

Would I read it again?   YES / NO

Would I recommend it?   YES / NO

If so, to whom? ....

....

Themes or characters that resonated with me: ....

....

Emotions, thoughts, or memories it brought up in me: ....

....

Opinion about the author or writing style: ....

....

MY RATINGS

WRITING STYLE	☆☆☆☆☆	READABILITY	☆☆☆☆☆
RELATABILITY	☆☆☆☆☆	PERSONAL IMPACT	☆☆☆☆☆
ORIGINALITY	☆☆☆☆☆	PLOT	☆☆☆☆☆
....	☆☆☆☆☆	....	☆☆☆☆☆
....	☆☆☆☆☆	....	☆☆☆☆☆
....	☆☆☆☆☆	....	☆☆☆☆☆

MY OVERALL RATING ☆☆☆☆☆

BOOK CLUB NOTES

MY BIGGEST TAKEAWAY

Title: ....

Author: ....

Genre: ....

Format: PAPER / DIGITAL / AUDIO

Recommended by/Why I'm reading it: ....

....

Date started: .... Date finished: ....

MY ANALYSIS

Would I read it again?   YES / NO

Would I recommend it?   YES / NO
If so, to whom? ....

....

Themes or characters that resonated with me: ....

....

Emotions, thoughts, or memories it brought up in me: ....

....

Opinion about the author or writing style: ....

....

MY RATINGS

WRITING STYLE	☆☆☆☆☆	READABILITY	☆☆☆☆☆
RELATABILITY	☆☆☆☆☆	PERSONAL IMPACT	☆☆☆☆☆
ORIGINALITY	☆☆☆☆☆	PLOT	☆☆☆☆☆
....	☆☆☆☆☆	....	☆☆☆☆☆
....	☆☆☆☆☆	....	☆☆☆☆☆
....	☆☆☆☆☆	....	☆☆☆☆☆

MY OVERALL RATING ☆☆☆☆☆

BOOK CLUB NOTES

MY BIGGEST TAKEAWAY

Title: ....

Author: ....

Genre: ....

Format: PAPER / DIGITAL / AUDIO

Recommended by/Why I'm reading it: ....

....

Date started: .... Date finished: ....

MY ANALYSIS

Would I read it again?   YES / NO

Would I recommend it?   YES / NO
If so, to whom? ....

....

Themes or characters that resonated with me: ....

....

Emotions, thoughts, or memories it brought up in me: ....

....

Opinion about the author or writing style: ....

....

MY RATINGS

WRITING STYLE	☆ ☆ ☆ ☆ ☆	READABILITY	☆ ☆ ☆ ☆ ☆
RELATABILITY	☆ ☆ ☆ ☆ ☆	PERSONAL IMPACT	☆ ☆ ☆ ☆ ☆
ORIGINALITY	☆ ☆ ☆ ☆ ☆	PLOT	☆ ☆ ☆ ☆ ☆
....	☆ ☆ ☆ ☆ ☆	....	☆ ☆ ☆ ☆ ☆
....	☆ ☆ ☆ ☆ ☆	....	☆ ☆ ☆ ☆ ☆
....	☆ ☆ ☆ ☆ ☆	....	☆ ☆ ☆ ☆ ☆

MY OVERALL RATING ☆ ☆ ☆ ☆ ☆

BOOK CLUB NOTES

MY BIGGEST TAKEAWAY

Title: ....

Author: ....

Genre: ....

Format: PAPER / DIGITAL / AUDIO

Recommended by/Why I'm reading it: ....

....

Date started: .... Date finished: ....

MY ANALYSIS

Would I read it again?   YES / NO

Would I recommend it?   YES / NO

If so, to whom? ....

....

Themes or characters that resonated with me: ....

....

Emotions, thoughts, or memories it brought up in me: ....

....

Opinion about the author or writing style: ....

....

MY RATINGS

WRITING STYLE	☆ ☆ ☆ ☆ ☆	READABILITY	☆ ☆ ☆ ☆ ☆
RELATABILITY	☆ ☆ ☆ ☆ ☆	PERSONAL IMPACT	☆ ☆ ☆ ☆ ☆
ORIGINALITY	☆ ☆ ☆ ☆ ☆	PLOT	☆ ☆ ☆ ☆ ☆
....	☆ ☆ ☆ ☆ ☆	....	☆ ☆ ☆ ☆ ☆
....	☆ ☆ ☆ ☆ ☆	....	☆ ☆ ☆ ☆ ☆
....	☆ ☆ ☆ ☆ ☆	....	☆ ☆ ☆ ☆ ☆

MY OVERALL RATING ☆ ☆ ☆ ☆ ☆

BOOK CLUB NOTES

MY BIGGEST TAKEAWAY

Title: ....

Author: ....

Genre: ....

Format: PAPER / DIGITAL / AUDIO

Recommended by/Why I'm reading it: ....

....

Date started: .... Date finished: ....

MY ANALYSIS

Would I read it again?   YES / NO

Would I recommend it?   YES / NO
If so, to whom? ....

....

Themes or characters that resonated with me: ....

....

Emotions, thoughts, or memories it brought up in me: ....

....

Opinion about the author or writing style: ....

....

MY RATINGS

WRITING STYLE	☆☆☆☆☆	READABILITY	☆☆☆☆☆
RELATABILITY	☆☆☆☆☆	PERSONAL IMPACT	☆☆☆☆☆
ORIGINALITY	☆☆☆☆☆	PLOT	☆☆☆☆☆
....	☆☆☆☆☆	....	☆☆☆☆☆
....	☆☆☆☆☆	....	☆☆☆☆☆
....	☆☆☆☆☆	....	☆☆☆☆☆

MY OVERALL RATING ☆☆☆☆☆

BOOK CLUB NOTES

MY BIGGEST TAKEAWAY

Title: ....

Author: ....

Genre: ....

Format: PAPER / DIGITAL / AUDIO

Recommended by/Why I'm reading it: ....

....

Date started: .... Date finished: ....

MY ANALYSIS

Would I read it again?   YES / NO

Would I recommend it?   YES / NO

If so, to whom? ....

....

Themes or characters that resonated with me: ....

....

Emotions, thoughts, or memories it brought up in me: ....

....

Opinion about the author or writing style: ....

....

MY RATINGS

WRITING STYLE	☆ ☆ ☆ ☆ ☆	READABILITY	☆ ☆ ☆ ☆ ☆
RELATABILITY	☆ ☆ ☆ ☆ ☆	PERSONAL IMPACT	☆ ☆ ☆ ☆ ☆
ORIGINALITY	☆ ☆ ☆ ☆ ☆	PLOT	☆ ☆ ☆ ☆ ☆
....	☆ ☆ ☆ ☆ ☆	....	☆ ☆ ☆ ☆ ☆
....	☆ ☆ ☆ ☆ ☆	....	☆ ☆ ☆ ☆ ☆
....	☆ ☆ ☆ ☆ ☆	....	☆ ☆ ☆ ☆ ☆

MY OVERALL RATING ☆ ☆ ☆ ☆ ☆

BOOK CLUB NOTES

MY BIGGEST TAKEAWAY

Title: ....

Author: ....

Genre: ....

Format: PAPER / DIGITAL / AUDIO

Recommended by/Why I'm reading it: ....

....

Date started: .... Date finished: ....

MY ANALYSIS

Would I read it again?   YES / NO

Would I recommend it?   YES / NO

If so, to whom? ....

....

Themes or characters that resonated with me: ....

....

Emotions, thoughts, or memories it brought up in me: ....

....

Opinion about the author or writing style: ....

....

MY RATINGS

WRITING STYLE	☆ ☆ ☆ ☆ ☆	READABILITY	☆ ☆ ☆ ☆ ☆
RELATABILITY	☆ ☆ ☆ ☆ ☆	PERSONAL IMPACT	☆ ☆ ☆ ☆ ☆
ORIGINALITY	☆ ☆ ☆ ☆ ☆	PLOT	☆ ☆ ☆ ☆ ☆
....	☆ ☆ ☆ ☆ ☆	....	☆ ☆ ☆ ☆ ☆
....	☆ ☆ ☆ ☆ ☆	....	☆ ☆ ☆ ☆ ☆
....	☆ ☆ ☆ ☆ ☆	....	☆ ☆ ☆ ☆ ☆

MY OVERALL RATING ☆ ☆ ☆ ☆ ☆

BOOK CLUB NOTES

MY BIGGEST TAKEAWAY

Title: ....

Author: ....

Genre: ....

Format: PAPER / DIGITAL / AUDIO

Recommended by/Why I'm reading it: ....

....

Date started: .... Date finished: ....

MY ANALYSIS

Would I read it again?   YES / NO

Would I recommend it?   YES / NO
If so, to whom? ....

....

Themes or characters that resonated with me: ....

....

Emotions, thoughts, or memories it brought up in me: ....

....

Opinion about the author or writing style: ....

....

MY RATINGS

WRITING STYLE	☆ ☆ ☆ ☆ ☆	READABILITY	☆ ☆ ☆ ☆ ☆
RELATABILITY	☆ ☆ ☆ ☆ ☆	PERSONAL IMPACT	☆ ☆ ☆ ☆ ☆
ORIGINALITY	☆ ☆ ☆ ☆ ☆	PLOT	☆ ☆ ☆ ☆ ☆
....	☆ ☆ ☆ ☆ ☆	....	☆ ☆ ☆ ☆ ☆
....	☆ ☆ ☆ ☆ ☆	....	☆ ☆ ☆ ☆ ☆
....	☆ ☆ ☆ ☆ ☆	....	☆ ☆ ☆ ☆ ☆

MY OVERALL RATING ☆ ☆ ☆ ☆ ☆

BOOK CLUB NOTES

MY BIGGEST TAKEAWAY

Title: ....

Author: ....

Genre: ....

Format: PAPER / DIGITAL / AUDIO

Recommended by/Why I'm reading it: ....

....

Date started: .... Date finished: ....

MY ANALYSIS

Would I read it again?   YES / NO

Would I recommend it?   YES / NO

If so, to whom? ....

Themes or characters that resonated with me: ....

Emotions, thoughts, or memories it brought up in me: ....

Opinion about the author or writing style: ....

....

MY RATINGS

WRITING STYLE	☆☆☆☆☆	READABILITY	☆☆☆☆☆
RELATABILITY	☆☆☆☆☆	PERSONAL IMPACT	☆☆☆☆☆
ORIGINALITY	☆☆☆☆☆	PLOT	☆☆☆☆☆
....	☆☆☆☆☆	....	☆☆☆☆☆
....	☆☆☆☆☆	....	☆☆☆☆☆
....	☆☆☆☆☆	....	☆☆☆☆☆

MY OVERALL RATING ☆☆☆☆☆

BOOK CLUB NOTES

MY BIGGEST TAKEAWAY

Title: ....

Author: ....

Genre: ....

Format: PAPER / DIGITAL / AUDIO

Recommended by/Why I'm reading it: ....
....

Date started: .... Date finished: ....

MY ANALYSIS

Would I read it again? YES / NO

Would I recommend it? YES / NO
If so, to whom? ....
....

Themes or characters that resonated with me: ....
....

Emotions, thoughts, or memories it brought up in me: ....
....

Opinion about the author or writing style: ....
....

MY RATINGS

WRITING STYLE	☆☆☆☆☆	READABILITY	☆☆☆☆☆
RELATABILITY	☆☆☆☆☆	PERSONAL IMPACT	☆☆☆☆☆
ORIGINALITY	☆☆☆☆☆	PLOT	☆☆☆☆☆
....	☆☆☆☆☆	....	☆☆☆☆☆
....	☆☆☆☆☆	....	☆☆☆☆☆
....	☆☆☆☆☆	....	☆☆☆☆☆

MY OVERALL RATING ☆☆☆☆☆

BOOK CLUB NOTES

MY BIGGEST TAKEAWAY

Title: ....

Author: ....

Genre: ....

Format: PAPER / DIGITAL / AUDIO

Recommended by/Why I'm reading it: ....
....

Date started: ....   Date finished: ....

MY ANALYSIS

Would I read it again?   YES / NO

Would I recommend it?   YES / NO
If so, to whom? ....

Themes or characters that resonated with me: ....
....

Emotions, thoughts, or memories it brought up in me: ....
....

Opinion about the author or writing style: ....
....

MY RATINGS

WRITING STYLE	☆ ☆ ☆ ☆ ☆	READABILITY	☆ ☆ ☆ ☆ ☆
RELATABILITY	☆ ☆ ☆ ☆ ☆	PERSONAL IMPACT	☆ ☆ ☆ ☆ ☆
ORIGINALITY	☆ ☆ ☆ ☆ ☆	PLOT	☆ ☆ ☆ ☆ ☆
....	☆ ☆ ☆ ☆ ☆	....	☆ ☆ ☆ ☆ ☆
....	☆ ☆ ☆ ☆ ☆	....	☆ ☆ ☆ ☆ ☆
....	☆ ☆ ☆ ☆ ☆	....	☆ ☆ ☆ ☆ ☆

MY OVERALL RATING ☆ ☆ ☆ ☆ ☆

BOOK CLUB NOTES

MY BIGGEST TAKEAWAY

Title: ....

Author: ....

Genre: ....

Format: PAPER / DIGITAL / AUDIO

Recommended by/Why I'm reading it: ....

....

Date started: .... Date finished: ....

MY ANALYSIS

Would I read it again?   YES / NO

Would I recommend it?   YES / NO
If so, to whom? ....

....

Themes or characters that resonated with me: ....

....

Emotions, thoughts, or memories it brought up in me: ....

....

Opinion about the author or writing style: ....

....

MY RATINGS

WRITING STYLE	☆☆☆☆☆	READABILITY	☆☆☆☆☆
RELATABILITY	☆☆☆☆☆	PERSONAL IMPACT	☆☆☆☆☆
ORIGINALITY	☆☆☆☆☆	PLOT	☆☆☆☆☆
....	☆☆☆☆☆	....	☆☆☆☆☆
....	☆☆☆☆☆	....	☆☆☆☆☆
....	☆☆☆☆☆	....	☆☆☆☆☆

MY OVERALL RATING ☆☆☆☆☆

BOOK CLUB NOTES

MY BIGGEST TAKEAWAY

Title: ....

Author: ....

Genre: ....

Format: PAPER / DIGITAL / AUDIO

Recommended by/Why I'm reading it: ....
....

Date started: .... Date finished: ....

MY ANALYSIS

Would I read it again?   YES / NO

Would I recommend it?   YES / NO
If so, to whom? ....
....

Themes or characters that resonated with me: ....
....

Emotions, thoughts, or memories it brought up in me: ......
....

Opinion about the author or writing style: ....
....

MY RATINGS

WRITING STYLE	☆☆☆☆☆	READABILITY	☆☆☆☆☆
RELATABILITY	☆☆☆☆☆	PERSONAL IMPACT	☆☆☆☆☆
ORIGINALITY	☆☆☆☆☆	PLOT	☆☆☆☆☆
....	☆☆☆☆☆	....	☆☆☆☆☆
....	☆☆☆☆☆	....	☆☆☆☆☆
....	☆☆☆☆☆	....	☆☆☆☆☆

MY OVERALL RATING ☆☆☆☆☆

BOOK CLUB NOTES

MY BIGGEST TAKEAWAY

Title: ....

Author: ....

Genre: ....

Format: PAPER / DIGITAL / AUDIO

Recommended by/Why I'm reading it: ....

....

Date started: .... Date finished: ....

MY ANALYSIS

Would I read it again? YES / NO

Would I recommend it? YES / NO
If so, to whom? ....

....

Themes or characters that resonated with me: ....

....

Emotions, thoughts, or memories it brought up in me: ....

....

Opinion about the author or writing style: ....

....

MY RATINGS

WRITING STYLE	☆☆☆☆☆	READABILITY	☆☆☆☆☆
RELATABILITY	☆☆☆☆☆	PERSONAL IMPACT	☆☆☆☆☆
ORIGINALITY	☆☆☆☆☆	PLOT	☆☆☆☆☆
....	☆☆☆☆☆	....	☆☆☆☆☆
....	☆☆☆☆☆	....	☆☆☆☆☆
....	☆☆☆☆☆	....	☆☆☆☆☆

MY OVERALL RATING ☆☆☆☆☆

BOOK CLUB NOTES

_____
_____
_____
_____
_____
_____
_____
_____
_____
_____
_____
_____
_____
_____
_____
_____
_____
_____
_____

MY BIGGEST TAKEAWAY

_____
_____
_____
_____
_____
_____

Title: ....

Author: ....

Genre: ....

Format: PAPER / DIGITAL / AUDIO

Recommended by/Why I'm reading it: ....

....

Date started: .... Date finished: ....

MY ANALYSIS

Would I read it again?   YES / NO

Would I recommend it?   YES / NO

If so, to whom? ....

....

Themes or characters that resonated with me: ....

....

Emotions, thoughts, or memories it brought up in me: ....

....

Opinion about the author or writing style: ....

....

MY RATINGS

WRITING STYLE	☆ ☆ ☆ ☆ ☆	READABILITY	☆ ☆ ☆ ☆ ☆
RELATABILITY	☆ ☆ ☆ ☆ ☆	PERSONAL IMPACT	☆ ☆ ☆ ☆ ☆
ORIGINALITY	☆ ☆ ☆ ☆ ☆	PLOT	☆ ☆ ☆ ☆ ☆
....	☆ ☆ ☆ ☆ ☆	....	☆ ☆ ☆ ☆ ☆
....	☆ ☆ ☆ ☆ ☆	....	☆ ☆ ☆ ☆ ☆
....	☆ ☆ ☆ ☆ ☆	....	☆ ☆ ☆ ☆ ☆

MY OVERALL RATING ☆ ☆ ☆ ☆ ☆

BOOK CLUB NOTES

MY BIGGEST TAKEAWAY

Title: ....

Author: ....

Genre: ....

Format: PAPER / DIGITAL / AUDIO

Recommended by/Why I'm reading it: ....

....

Date started: .... Date finished: ....

MY ANALYSIS

Would I read it again?   YES / NO

Would I recommend it?   YES / NO

If so, to whom? ....

....

Themes or characters that resonated with me: ....

....

Emotions, thoughts, or memories it brought up in me: ......

....

Opinion about the author or writing style: ....

....

MY RATINGS

WRITING STYLE	☆☆☆☆☆	READABILITY	☆☆☆☆☆
RELATABILITY	☆☆☆☆☆	PERSONAL IMPACT	☆☆☆☆☆
ORIGINALITY	☆☆☆☆☆	PLOT	☆☆☆☆☆
....	☆☆☆☆☆	....	☆☆☆☆☆
....	☆☆☆☆☆	....	☆☆☆☆☆
....	☆☆☆☆☆	....	☆☆☆☆☆

MY OVERALL RATING ☆☆☆☆☆

BOOK CLUB NOTES

MY BIGGEST TAKEAWAY

Title: ....

Author: ....

Genre: ....

Format: PAPER / DIGITAL / AUDIO

Recommended by/Why I'm reading it: ....

....

Date started: .... Date finished: ....

MY ANALYSIS

Would I read it again? YES / NO

Would I recommend it? YES / NO
If so, to whom? ....

....

Themes or characters that resonated with me: ....

....

Emotions, thoughts, or memories it brought up in me: ....

....

Opinion about the author or writing style: ....

....

MY RATINGS

WRITING STYLE	☆ ☆ ☆ ☆ ☆	READABILITY	☆ ☆ ☆ ☆ ☆
RELATABILITY	☆ ☆ ☆ ☆ ☆	PERSONAL IMPACT	☆ ☆ ☆ ☆ ☆
ORIGINALITY	☆ ☆ ☆ ☆ ☆	PLOT	☆ ☆ ☆ ☆ ☆
....	☆ ☆ ☆ ☆ ☆	....	☆ ☆ ☆ ☆ ☆
....	☆ ☆ ☆ ☆ ☆	....	☆ ☆ ☆ ☆ ☆
....	☆ ☆ ☆ ☆ ☆	....	☆ ☆ ☆ ☆ ☆

MY OVERALL RATING ☆ ☆ ☆ ☆ ☆

BOOK CLUB NOTES

MY BIGGEST TAKEAWAY

Title: ....

Author: ....

Genre: ....

Format: PAPER / DIGITAL / AUDIO

Recommended by/Why I'm reading it: ....
....

Date started: .... Date finished: ....

MY ANALYSIS

Would I read it again?   YES / NO

Would I recommend it?   YES / NO

If so, to whom? ....
....

Themes or characters that resonated with me: ....
....

Emotions, thoughts, or memories it brought up in me: ....
....

Opinion about the author or writing style: ....
....
....

MY RATINGS

WRITING STYLE	☆☆☆☆☆	READABILITY	☆☆☆☆☆
RELATABILITY	☆☆☆☆☆	PERSONAL IMPACT	☆☆☆☆☆
ORIGINALITY	☆☆☆☆☆	PLOT	☆☆☆☆☆
....	☆☆☆☆☆	....	☆☆☆☆☆
....	☆☆☆☆☆	....	☆☆☆☆☆
....	☆☆☆☆☆	....	☆☆☆☆☆

MY OVERALL RATING ☆☆☆☆☆

BOOK CLUB NOTES

MY BIGGEST TAKEAWAY

Title: ....

Author: ....

Genre: ....

Format: PAPER / DIGITAL / AUDIO

Recommended by/Why I'm reading it: ....

....

Date started: ....   Date finished: ....

MY ANALYSIS

Would I read it again?   YES / NO

Would I recommend it?   YES / NO
If so, to whom? ....

....

Themes or characters that resonated with me: ....

....

Emotions, thoughts, or memories it brought up in me: ....

....

Opinion about the author or writing style: ....

....

MY RATINGS

WRITING STYLE	☆ ☆ ☆ ☆ ☆	READABILITY	☆ ☆ ☆ ☆ ☆
RELATABILITY	☆ ☆ ☆ ☆ ☆	PERSONAL IMPACT	☆ ☆ ☆ ☆ ☆
ORIGINALITY	☆ ☆ ☆ ☆ ☆	PLOT	☆ ☆ ☆ ☆ ☆
....	☆ ☆ ☆ ☆ ☆	....	☆ ☆ ☆ ☆ ☆
....	☆ ☆ ☆ ☆ ☆	....	☆ ☆ ☆ ☆ ☆
....	☆ ☆ ☆ ☆ ☆	....	☆ ☆ ☆ ☆ ☆

MY OVERALL RATING ☆ ☆ ☆ ☆ ☆

BOOK CLUB NOTES

_____
_____
_____
_____
_____
_____
_____
_____
_____
_____
_____
_____
_____
_____
_____
_____
_____
_____
_____
_____

MY BIGGEST TAKEAWAY

_____
_____
_____
_____
_____
_____

Title: ....

Author: ....

Genre: ....

Format: PAPER / DIGITAL / AUDIO

Recommended by/Why I'm reading it: ....

....

Date started: .... Date finished: ....

MY ANALYSIS

Would I read it again?   YES / NO

Would I recommend it?   YES / NO

If so, to whom? ....

....

Themes or characters that resonated with me: ....

....

Emotions, thoughts, or memories it brought up in me: ....

....

Opinion about the author or writing style: ....

....

MY RATINGS

WRITING STYLE	☆☆☆☆☆	READABILITY	☆☆☆☆☆
RELATABILITY	☆☆☆☆☆	PERSONAL IMPACT	☆☆☆☆☆
ORIGINALITY	☆☆☆☆☆	PLOT	☆☆☆☆☆
....	☆☆☆☆☆	....	☆☆☆☆☆
....	☆☆☆☆☆	....	☆☆☆☆☆
....	☆☆☆☆☆	....	☆☆☆☆☆

MY OVERALL RATING ☆☆☆☆☆

BOOK CLUB NOTES

MY BIGGEST TAKEAWAY

Title: ....

Author: ....

Genre: ....

Format: PAPER / DIGITAL / AUDIO

Recommended by/Why I'm reading it: ....
....

Date started: .... Date finished: ....

MY ANALYSIS

Would I read it again?   YES / NO

Would I recommend it?   YES / NO
If so, to whom? ....

Themes or characters that resonated with me: ....

Emotions, thoughts, or memories it brought up in me: ....

Opinion about the author or writing style: ....
....

MY RATINGS

WRITING STYLE	☆ ☆ ☆ ☆ ☆	READABILITY	☆ ☆ ☆ ☆ ☆
RELATABILITY	☆ ☆ ☆ ☆ ☆	PERSONAL IMPACT	☆ ☆ ☆ ☆ ☆
ORIGINALITY	☆ ☆ ☆ ☆ ☆	PLOT	☆ ☆ ☆ ☆ ☆
....	☆ ☆ ☆ ☆ ☆	....	☆ ☆ ☆ ☆ ☆
....	☆ ☆ ☆ ☆ ☆	....	☆ ☆ ☆ ☆ ☆
....	☆ ☆ ☆ ☆ ☆	....	☆ ☆ ☆ ☆ ☆

MY OVERALL RATING ☆ ☆ ☆ ☆ ☆

BOOK CLUB NOTES

MY BIGGEST TAKEAWAY

Title: ....

Author: ....

Genre: ....

Format: PAPER / DIGITAL / AUDIO

Recommended by/Why I'm reading it: ....

....

Date started: .... Date finished: ....

MY ANALYSIS

Would I read it again?   YES / NO

Would I recommend it?   YES / NO
If so, to whom? ....

....

Themes or characters that resonated with me: ....

....

Emotions, thoughts, or memories it brought up in me: ....

....

Opinion about the author or writing style: ....

....

MY RATINGS

WRITING STYLE	☆☆☆☆☆	READABILITY	☆☆☆☆☆
RELATABILITY	☆☆☆☆☆	PERSONAL IMPACT	☆☆☆☆☆
ORIGINALITY	☆☆☆☆☆	PLOT	☆☆☆☆☆
....	☆☆☆☆☆	....	☆☆☆☆☆
....	☆☆☆☆☆	....	☆☆☆☆☆
....	☆☆☆☆☆	....	☆☆☆☆☆

MY OVERALL RATING ☆☆☆☆☆

BOOK CLUB NOTES

MY BIGGEST TAKEAWAY

Title: ....

Author: ....

Genre: ....

Format: PAPER / DIGITAL / AUDIO

Recommended by/Why I'm reading it: ....

....

Date started: .... Date finished: ....

MY ANALYSIS

Would I read it again?   YES / NO

Would I recommend it?   YES / NO
If so, to whom? ....

....

Themes or characters that resonated with me: ....

....

Emotions, thoughts, or memories it brought up in me: ....

....

Opinion about the author or writing style: ....

....

MY RATINGS

WRITING STYLE	☆ ☆ ☆ ☆ ☆	READABILITY	☆ ☆ ☆ ☆ ☆
RELATABILITY	☆ ☆ ☆ ☆ ☆	PERSONAL IMPACT	☆ ☆ ☆ ☆ ☆
ORIGINALITY	☆ ☆ ☆ ☆ ☆	PLOT	☆ ☆ ☆ ☆ ☆
....	☆ ☆ ☆ ☆ ☆	....	☆ ☆ ☆ ☆ ☆
....	☆ ☆ ☆ ☆ ☆	....	☆ ☆ ☆ ☆ ☆
....	☆ ☆ ☆ ☆ ☆	....	☆ ☆ ☆ ☆ ☆

MY OVERALL RATING ☆ ☆ ☆ ☆ ☆

BOOK CLUB NOTES

MY BIGGEST TAKEAWAY

Title: ....

Author: ....

Genre: ....

Format: PAPER / DIGITAL / AUDIO

Recommended by/Why I'm reading it: ....

....

Date started: .... Date finished: ....

MY ANALYSIS

Would I read it again?   YES / NO

Would I recommend it?   YES / NO
If so, to whom? ....

....

Themes or characters that resonated with me: ....

....

Emotions, thoughts, or memories it brought up in me: ....

....

Opinion about the author or writing style: ....

....

MY RATINGS

WRITING STYLE	☆ ☆ ☆ ☆ ☆	READABILITY	☆ ☆ ☆ ☆ ☆
RELATABILITY	☆ ☆ ☆ ☆ ☆	PERSONAL IMPACT	☆ ☆ ☆ ☆ ☆
ORIGINALITY	☆ ☆ ☆ ☆ ☆	PLOT	☆ ☆ ☆ ☆ ☆
....	☆ ☆ ☆ ☆ ☆	....	☆ ☆ ☆ ☆ ☆
....	☆ ☆ ☆ ☆ ☆	....	☆ ☆ ☆ ☆ ☆
....	☆ ☆ ☆ ☆ ☆	....	☆ ☆ ☆ ☆ ☆

MY OVERALL RATING ☆ ☆ ☆ ☆ ☆

BOOK CLUB NOTES

MY BIGGEST TAKEAWAY

Title: ....

Author: ....

Genre: ....

Format: PAPER / DIGITAL / AUDIO

Recommended by/Why I'm reading it: ....
....

Date started: .... Date finished: ....

MY ANALYSIS

Would I read it again?   YES / NO

Would I recommend it?   YES / NO
If so, to whom? ....
....

Themes or characters that resonated with me: ....
....

Emotions, thoughts, or memories it brought up in me: ......
....

Opinion about the author or writing style: ....
....

MY RATINGS

WRITING STYLE	☆ ☆ ☆ ☆ ☆	READABILITY	☆ ☆ ☆ ☆ ☆
RELATABILITY	☆ ☆ ☆ ☆ ☆	PERSONAL IMPACT	☆ ☆ ☆ ☆ ☆
ORIGINALITY	☆ ☆ ☆ ☆ ☆	PLOT	☆ ☆ ☆ ☆ ☆
....	☆ ☆ ☆ ☆ ☆	....	☆ ☆ ☆ ☆ ☆
....	☆ ☆ ☆ ☆ ☆	....	☆ ☆ ☆ ☆ ☆
....	☆ ☆ ☆ ☆ ☆	....	☆ ☆ ☆ ☆ ☆

MY OVERALL RATING ☆ ☆ ☆ ☆ ☆

BOOK CLUB NOTES

_____
_____
_____
_____
_____
_____
_____
_____
_____
_____
_____
_____
_____
_____
_____
_____
_____
_____

MY BIGGEST TAKEAWAY

_____
_____
_____
_____
_____

MAKING THE MOST OF YOUR BOOK CLUB EXPERIENCE

HOW TO READ A BOOK FOR DISCUSSION

When you're reading a good book, it's easy to fly through the pages and get lost in the story. While that's certainly one way to read and enjoy a book, it can make it hard to talk about the book later in a discussion format. Reading a book for discussion requires a certain amount of awareness, attention to detail, and objectivity. Here are some tips for reading in a way that helps you participate more fully in a book club discussion:

♦ Before you dive into the story, take a minute to focus on yourself and what interests you about this book, and then try to read slowly and thoughtfully. Noticing details will help you remember the book better in the long term and will give you great talking points in the upcoming book club conversation.

♦ Refer to the list of Sample Discussion Questions beginning on page 252 before you start reading. Pick out a few questions that interest you, and as you read, take mental notes of ideas, quotes, scenes, and character traits that are relevant to those questions.

♦ Write down your observations in the Book Club Notes section of your journal page. Remember important passages later on by jotting down page numbers near relevant notes on your journal page, using sticky notes to flag book pages, or bookmarking ebook pages.

Don't get bogged down taking pages of notes or trying to dissect the story like you're in school—just keep track of some key points so you're able to reference them during your get-together.

CONVERSATION GUIDELINES

Every book club needs a little help staying on topic every once in a while. The following is a sampling of discussion guidelines that your group might want to consider, based on the context, purpose, and demographics of your group.

- **Avoid interrupting and/or having side conversations.**
  Introducing related information about the author, setting, or historical background can be helpful but, in general, keep to the book and the current question under consideration.

- **Voice disagreements freely but respectfully.**
  Bringing up a contrasting perspective is perfectly acceptable, as long as members stay even-keeled and curious, instead of oppositional.

- **Participate.**
  Some members are probably naturally going to be more vocal than others. Even if you're on the quieter side, though, don't be afraid to share your thoughts and comments.

- **Invite opinions.**
  The purpose of a book club is to have conversations, so try to voice your opinions in an open-ended way that invites input. For example, say "I wonder if...," or "I felt_____, so I'm curious about how everyone else felt." And so on.

- **Be an active listener.**
  Engage with what the speaker is saying. Ask questions or rephrase their statements if you don't understand where they are coming from.

It's okay if it takes some trial and error to find what guidelines work best for your group and for creating the environment you want.

EXPANDING YOUR BOOK CLUB

If your book club is looking to add a few members, there are lots of ways to go about it. Here are some easy ideas:

♦ Have current or former club members invite or recommend friends to join the group.

♦ Consider changing the time or venue to be more accommodating to the majority of members' schedules.

♦ Use an online platform like *Goodreads* to start a public or private group, and invite people who don't live near you.

Your group's membership might grow or shrink periodically, but that's all right. Keep the overall experience fun and entertaining, and your group is sure to be successful.

RECOMMENDED READING LISTS

CLASSICS

1 **To Kill a Mockingbird** by HARPER LEE

The 1961 Pulitzer Prize–winning novel giving a child's view of race and justice in the Depression-era South. Masterful storytelling on themes still relevant today.

2 **The Great Gatsby** by F. SCOTT FITZGERALD

The tragic story of Jay Gatsby, an eccentric, self-made millionaire and his pursuit of wealthy young Daisy Buchanan.

3 **The Scarlet Pimpernel** by BARONESS ORCZY

A colorful romantic classic set during the French Revolution in which a mysterious English nobleman known as the Scarlet Pimpernel snatches French aristocrats from the jaws of the guillotine.

4 **Jane Eyre** by CHARLOTTE BRONTË

Orphan Jane Eyre endures harsh relatives, an inhumane boarding school, torturous secrets, and heartbreak before finding a home and true love.

5 **1984** by GEORGE ORWELL

A dystopian tale in which Winston Smith and his lover Julia fight for freedom against the hegemonic mind control of the state.

6 **One Hundred Years of Solitude** by GABRIEL GARCÍA MÁRQUEZ

The once-peaceful, isolated town of Macondo and its founding family, the Buendías, undergo drastic changes as they begin to mingle with surrounding cultures. Will its former magical charm ever be restored?

7 *Tarzan of the Apes* by EDGAR RICE BURROUGHS

The iconic story of a baby raised by a tribe of apes and his subsequent romantic-yet-tragic reentry into human society.

8 *Catch-22* by JOSEPH HELLER

A satirical novel chronicling freewheeling American bombardier John Yossarian's attempts to avoid combat and stay alive during World War II.

9 *Slaughterhouse-Five* by KURT VONNEGUT

An anti-war classic, complete with sci-fi elements, about POW Billy Pilgrim's time-and-space travel escapades.

10 *The Brothers Karamazov* by FYODOR DOSTOEVSKY

A family tragedy tracing the lives of three brothers wrestling with life, meaning, humanity, and God.

11 *The Sun Also Rises* by ERNEST HEMINGWAY

Narrator Jake Barnes recounts the travels, romances, and travails of a band of disillusioned expatriates living in post–World War I Europe.

12 *The Handmaid's Tale* by MARGARET ATWOOD

The dystopian society Gilead, threatened by low reproduction rates, enslaves women as surrogates or "Handmaids." This is the tale of the Handmaid Offred and her companions.

13 *Atlas Shrugged* by AYN RAND

A futuristic tale of mystery, murder, leadership, and the triumph of the human mind and spirit.

14 *The Count of Monte Cristo* by ALEXANDRE DUMAS

The timeless saga of Edmond Dantès's love, jealousy, unjust imprisonment, escape, and quest for revenge.

15 *Pride and Prejudice* by JANE AUSTEN

The quintessential Georgian romantic novel of manners tells the story of Elizabeth Bennet and her sisters' economic distress and their quests for marriage.

CLASSICS, *CONTINUED*

16 *Frankenstein* by MARY SHELLEY

An early horror novel in which the protagonist, Victor Frankenstein, a grief-stricken young scientist in Geneva, creates the Monster, a murderous and hideously ugly, yet intelligent and sensitive, being.

17 *Fahrenheit 451* by RAY BRADBURY

In a dystopian society that forbids and burns books, Guy Montag discovers a stash of books that leads him to transformation and ignites a societal revolution.

18 *Anne of Green Gables* by L.M. MONTGOMERY

The orphanage sends a young girl, Anne Shirley, to the aging owners of Green Gables farm instead of the boy they had requested. Despite a rocky introduction, Anne and her optimistic spirit change the farm and the whole town of Avonlea forever.

19 *A Tale of Two Cities* by CHARLES DICKENS

A classic Dickens novel, split between London and Paris in the late eighteenth century, providing historical commentary and urging social reform via the story of the Manette family's tragedy.

20 *The Stranger* by ALBERT CAMUS

An exploration of absurdity and the apparent meaninglessness of life. This classic novel follows the life of main character Meursault from the time he receives news of his mother's death until his execution as a criminal.

21 *A Confederacy of Dunces* by JOHN KENNEDY TOOLE

Earning a posthumous Pulitzer Prize for Toole, *Confederacy* traces the tragicomic life of the eccentric and indolent Ignatius J. Reilly of New Orleans.

22 *The Master and Margarita* by MIKHAIL BULGAKOV

A Russian masterpiece set primarily in Moscow in the 1930s that blends multiple genres, including fantasy, farce, and romance.

23 *Mrs. Dalloway* by VIRGINIA WOOLF

A day in the life of upper-class wife and mother Clarissa Dalloway that brings her face to face with her past and forces her to reconsider her future.

24 *Les Misérables* by VICTOR HUGO

Themes of law and grace, justice and mercy run richly throughout this French classic about ex-convict Jean Valjean, whose character has been transformed, although figures from his past continue to torment him.

25 *War and Peace* by LEO TOLSTOY

A remarkable study in human nature, this story takes place during Napoleon's invasion of Russia and follows the lives of two men and the noblewoman they both love.

26 *The Godfather* by MARIO PUZO

A crime novel set immediately after World War II and featuring the rise and fall of the Corleone family and the New York mafia wars.

27 *The Adventures of Huckleberry Finn* by MARK TWAIN

The inimitable American author's tale of the roguish, endearing Huck Finn, a poor boy escaping from his abusive father, and his companion, the runaway slave Jim, as they voyage down the Mississippi River on a raft.

28 *The Jungle Book* by RUDYARD KIPLING

A collection of short stories about Mowgli, an Indian boy raised by wolves who learns wisdom and self-sufficiency from the jungle animals; a cobra-killing mongoose named Rikki-Tikki-Tavi; and other jungle legends.

29 *Michael Strogoff* by JULES VERNE

The spellbinding story of a courier for the czar, Michael Strogoff, who journeys across Russia to deliver a message to the czar's brother during the Tartars' invasion of Siberia.

30 *Their Eyes Were Watching God* by ZORA NEALE HURSTON

After a lifelong search for true love, Janie Crawford returns to her Florida hometown to tell her story.

MODERN BESTSELLERS

1 *Where the Crawdads Sing* by DELIA OWENS

When Chase Andrews's dead body is discovered, people in the small town of Barkley Cove on the North Carolina coast accuse gentle but reclusive Kya Clark, the "Marsh Girl," of murder. Will she be able to vindicate herself?

2 *The Institute* by STEPHEN KING

Twelve-year-old Luke is abducted and taken to a Maine "institute" for other gifted children (who have also been abducted), where his captors try to extract his paranormal powers and use them for evil.

3 *The Overstory* by RICHARD POWERS

Nine Americans—each with their own unique history and relationship with trees—must overcome change, the police, and tragedy to protect the trees they all love.

4 *Sing, Unburied, Sing* by JESMYN WARD

In this road novel and journey through Mississippi's past and present, the narrative shifts between thirteen-year-old Jojo and his mother Leonie to provide a window into a family's search for life, forgiveness, home, and freedom from death's haunting presence.

5 *Autumn* by ALI SMITH

Elisabeth Demand, a thirty-two-year-old art lecturer, faces the death of her elderly friend and mentor, discovers new connections with her single mother, and wrestles with the breakdown of human decency in her village amid the anti-immigrant fervor of post-Brexit Britain.

6 *Exit West* by MOHSIN HAMID

In a near-future dystopia, Nadia and Saeed escape from their war-torn city through a magical portal system that ends up landing them in refugee camps and other traumatizing circumstances. Will the doors ever lead to peace? Will their love survive?

7 *Daughter of Fortune* by ISABEL ALLENDE

Orphan Eliza Sommers follows Joaquín Andieta, the gold-seeking father of her unborn child, away from their native Chile to Northern California and the California gold rush. In her search for Joaquín, she finds her own path to transformation and personal freedom.

8 *The Alchemist* by PAULO COELHO

A recurring dream moves Santiago to leave his life as a shepherd in Andalusia to seek treasure at the Egyptian pyramids. His subsequent discovery of alchemy launches him into an even greater quest.

9 *The House of Broken Angels* by LUIS ALBERTO URREA

In this novel about a Mexican-American family, Big Angel is dying of cancer, but his family and final days are chock-full of the joy of life and gratitude for love and living.

10 *The Magicians* by LEV GROSSMAN

Teenager Quentin Coldwater is admitted to a secret college of magic in upstate New York, where he studies the complicated and difficult curriculum of modern sorcery, and eventually discovers the fantasy world of Fillory.

11 *Before We Were Yours* by LISA WINGATE

Based on the true story of a Memphis adoption agency that kidnapped and sold poor children to wealthy parents, this novel juxtaposes the narratives of twelve-year-old Rill Foss, a poor girl kidnapped in 1939, and Avery Stafford, a young, talented federal prosecutor in the present who uncovers a family mystery.

12 *Erasure* by PERCIVAL EVERETT

In this novel within a novel, professor and writer Monk Ellison becomes famous when his satirical work, written to parody the stereotypical story about the black experience in America, is accidently published without his knowledge.

13 *The Silent Patient* by ALEX MICHAELIDES

Criminal psychotherapist Theo Faber's work with Alicia Berenson, a famous painter who killed her husband and now refuses to speak a single word, threatens to upend his own stability.

14 *Such a Fun Age* by KILEY REID

Alix Chamberlain, self-made white businesswoman, becomes obsessed with her daughter's black babysitter, college graduate Emira Tucker, after Emira is accused of kidnapping Alix's two-year-old daughter. The drama that ensues changes their relationship and alters their self-perceptions forever.

15 *Gilead* by MARILYNNE ROBINSON

In this 2005 Pulitzer Prize–winning novel set in Iowa, John Ames, an old Congregationalist minister dying of heart disease, wrestles with forgiveness and writes his family history and reflections on life in a letter to his young son.

16 *The Whistler* by JOHN GRISHAM

Lacy Stoltz, legal investigator for the Florida Board on Judicial Conduct, gets assigned to a case involving a dirty judge skimming profits from a casino built on Native American land. As it turns out, this case might be the end of her career. And her life.

17 *Eleanor Oliphant Is Completely Fine* by GAIL HONEYMAN

Eccentric and solitary, Eleanor Oliphant is a Glasgow finance clerk whose social priorities begin to shift when she develops a crush on a local singer, Johnnie Lomond. Her later disillusionment and despair, coupled with the kindness of a coworker, open the path to personal healing for Eleanor.

18 *There There* by TOMMY ORANGE

The interwoven stories of twelve Native Americans in California who wrestle with the legacy of the multigenerational abuses and injustices they've suffered as Native Americans. A local powwow brings together their divergent stories.

19 *Then She Was Gone* by LISA JEWELL

The disappearance of beautiful and intelligent fifteen-year-old Ellie Mack from her London neighborhood leaves her mother Laurel and the rest of her family heartbroken. Ten years later, Laurel, now divorced, meets Floyd and his nine-year-old daughter, filling her with questions about what really happened to Ellie.

20 *Fool* by CHRISTOPHER MOORE

A modern satirical take on Shakespeare's *King Lear*, this story is told from the point of view of King Lear's jester, Pocket, and centers around Lear's three marriageable daughters.

21 *Shadow Music* by JULIE GARWOOD

The raw courage and sense of justice Scottish princess Gabrielle of St. Biel possesses land her in the middle of a Highland war under the scrutiny of warrior Colm MacHugh, the most feared man in Scotland.

22 *The Poet* by MICHAEL CONNELLY

When crime-beat reporter Jack McEvoy begins investigating the supposed suicide of his twin brother, a homicide detective, he finds himself in a fight for his life against a rogue FBI agent.

23 *Truly Madly Guilty* by LIANE MORIARTY

Family relationships and long-standing friendships begin to unravel following an unfortunate event at an impromptu neighborhood barbecue.

24 *The Black Widow* by DANIEL SILVA

In this fast-moving thriller, intelligence agent and art restorer Gabriel Allon receives a long-deserved promotion to lead Israel's intelligence service, but an ISIS attack in Paris pulls him back into the field for the darkest case he's ever handled.

25 *Night Circus* by ERIN MORGENSTERN

At a mysterious circus that opens only at night, two rival magicians and two children are drawn together by a magical bond greater than anyone could have foreseen.

26 *The Plot Against America* by PHILIP ROTH

An alternative history novel in which Charles Lindbergh wins the 1940 presidential election, signs a treaty with Hitler, and unleashes anti-Semitism in the US.

27 *The Tattooist of Auschwitz* by HEATHER MORRIS

Based on the true story of Lale Sokolov, a Jewish man who uses his role as the concentration camp tattooist to save lives, including that of Gita, his future wife.

28 *The Sky Is Yours* by CHANDLER KLANG SMITH

A mind-bending, futuristic fantasy novel set in the fictional city of Empire Island that tells the story of three teenagers learning to survive on their own in a decaying metropolis tormented by a pair of dragons.

29 *The Help* by KATHRYN STOCKETT

How three courageous women in 1962 Jackson, Mississippi, form a surprising and subversive partnership to fight segregation and racial injustice.

30 *Middlesex* by JEFFREY EUGENIDES

A Pulitzer Prize–winner set in Greece and Michigan in the twentieth century, this novel borrows heavily from Greek mythology and explores gender identity through the coming of age of protagonist Callie/Cal Stephanides.

BOOKS WRITTEN BY WOMEN

1 *The Clockmaker's Daughter* by KATE MORTON

If you like ghost stories, this novel is for you. A mysterious picture, a beautiful necklace, a murder, a nameless girl, and two unsuitable lovers are all somehow linked to Birchwood Manor, a country house on the Thames.

2 *And Then There Were None* by AGATHA CHRISTIE

Ten people invited to a party on an isolated island off the Devon coast of England followed by ten gruesome deaths—the quintessential murder mystery by a master of the genre. Avoid reading at bedtime.

3 *A Girl Is a Half-Formed Thing* by EIMEAR MCBRIDE

With all the mystique and melancholy of its Irish setting, this novel follows the traumatic, fragmented, and unsettling coming-of-age journey of a girl from an abusive home.

4 *My Year of Rest and Relaxation* by OTTESSA MOSHFEGH

In an effort to sleep for a year and avoid life, a recent Columbia graduate who seems to have a picture-perfect life gets intentionally hooked on antidepressants and other medications.

5 *Beloved* by TONI MORRISON

The devastating effects of slavery continue to haunt Sethe and her family years after they escape to Ohio to find their "freedom." A heartbreaking look at the legacy of slavery.

6 **The Broken Earth Trilogy** by N.K. JEMISIN

A futuristic series set on Stillness, a continent wracked by merciless Fifth Seasons that sweep in and reshape life and culture.

7 ***The Awakening*** by **KATE CHOPIN**

While vacationing at a resort on Grand Isle that is popular with wealthy New Orleans families, wife and mother Edna Pontellier forms new friendships that spur her search for personal freedom and open her up to a whole new way of life.

8 ***The Beggar Maid*** by **ALICE MUNRO**

In a series of chronological short stories, Munro tells the story of two conflicted family members: Rose, a working-class undergraduate who is in a relationship with well-to-do Patrick, and her stepmother, Flo, who is scornful of her stepdaughter's ambitions.

9 ***The Violent Bear It Away*** by **FLANNERY O'CONNOR**

In this Southern gothic novel, fourteen-year-old Francis Marion Tarwater tries to get away from his religious past but ultimately can't escape his prophetic calling and destiny.

10 ***All the Crooked Saints*** by **MAGGIE STIEFVATER**

Miracles and saints are part of the Soria family's legacy, but the pilgrims who come to the Sorias in Bicho Raro, Colorado, are often surprised by how miracles look in real life.

11 ***The Power*** by **NAOMI ALDERMAN**

When women develop the ability to release electricity through their fingertips and flip the power dynamic with men, their rise to power and potential to abuse it upends society.

12 ***Gun Dealers' Daughter*** by **GINA APOSTOL**

Soledad Soliman recounts the story of her transformation from a rich, aloof bookworm and daughter of a gun dealer to a Communist activist in Marcos-era Manila. In the process, she confronts her own checkered life, and reflects on the troubled history of the Philippines and its relationship with the US.

13 ***Difficult Women*** by **ROXANE GAY**

A collection of short stories about women from all backgrounds of life navigating the complex, cruel, and sometimes beautiful planet we call home.

14 *Fledgling* by OCTAVIA E. BUTLER

A human-vampire hybrid, Shori battles discrimination, poverty, sexism, and her own trauma in her quest for freedom and agency.

15 *Swing Time* by ZADIE SMITH

Tracey and her friend, the story's nameless narrator, both want to escape their London housing estates and become dancers, but fortune seemingly smiles only on the confident and talented Tracey, thus creating ongoing tension in a once close relationship.

16 *Rubyfruit Jungle* by RITA MAE BROWN

Molly, the adopted daughter of Carl and Carrie Bolt, discovers her lesbian identity in high school and experiences the hardship of having to make her own way in the world while pursuing her dream of making films.

17 *Autobiography of Red* by ANNE CARSON

Greek mythology shines through in this modern poem/novel about Geryon, a winged, red boy-monster, and his tumultuous relationship with his friend Herakles.

18 *The Future of Another Timeline* by ANNALEE NEWITZ

A feminist sci-fi novel in which Beth and Tess travel through time, battle misogynistic rivals, and rewrite history.

19 *The Good Luck Girls* by CHARLOTTE NICOLE DAVIS

In this dystopian tale, when Clementine accidently kills a man, her quick-thinking sister and friends turn the incident into an intrepid bid for freedom and escape from their life of slavery.

20 *Sick Kids in Love* by HANNAH MOSKOWITZ

Isabel's chronic illness informs her self-imposed rule: no dating. But Sasha has a chronic illness too. And he's in love with her. Should she break her rule?

21 *The Nest* by CYNTHIA D'APRIX SWEENEY

Four adult siblings grapple with their shared legacy of dysfunction as well as their own individual demons. Hanging in the balance is their inheritance, along with their family relationships and future.

22 *Everything We Keep* by KERRY LONSDALE

Sous chef Aimee attends her fiancé James's funeral on the day that was supposed to be their wedding day. But a psychic tells her that he is still alive—and her own heart confirms this. Her search for the truth about their life together begins.

23 *The Last Samurai* by HELEN DEWITT

Sibylla, an intellectual single mother living in a London flat, educates Ludo, her unusually gifted son, to prepare him for his quest to find his father.

24 *How Should a Person Be?* by SHEILA HETI

In this fictional portrait of a young artist, Sheila, surrounded by assorted artist friends and lovers, wrestles with the ethics of art and with her own sense of personhood and morality.

25 *The Particular Sadness of Lemon Cake* by AIMEE BENDER

On the cusp of her ninth birthday, Rose Edelstein discovers that she has a magical gift: She can taste emotions through food. At first, Rose considers this knowledge a shameful burden, but later discovers that other members of her family may have their own magical abilities.

26 *The Goldfinch* by DONNA TARTT

Winner of the 2014 Pulitzer Prize, this novel tells the story of thirteen-year-old Theo Decker—a boy who survived the accident that took his mother's life—and the small painting she left behind that entangles him in a web of mystery and danger.

27 *Wise Children* by ANGELA CARTER

Dora and Nora Chance are twin sisters from an eccentric theatrical family full of drama, twins, affairs, and well-kept secrets. With overtones of Shakespeare, this is a rich, relatable comedy.

28 *The Color Purple* by ALICE WALKER

In a series of letters stretching across twenty years, Celie writes to God and to her sister Nettie, chronicling her father's rapes, her subsequent pregnancies and loss of the babies, a forced and abusive marriage, friendships that offer a new way of life, and her final freedom and healing.

29 *The Need* by HELEN PHILLIPS

Molly is the lonely, socially isolated mother of two children who is being tormented by intrusive fears about her children's safety—and by a real or imagined doppelganger, Moll.

30 *Normal People* by SALLY ROONEY

Connell Waldron and Marianne Sheridan are two teenagers from different social and economic classes in County Sligo, Ireland, trying to figure out themselves, their world, and each other as they experience first love, school drama, family complexities, and social stigma.

BOOKS BY DIVERSE VOICES

1 *In the Time of the Butterflies* by JULIA ALVAREZ

Based on the true story of the Mirabal sisters, this historical novel is about four smart, courageous sisters from the Dominican Republic, known as the "butterflies," who become political revolutionaries.

2 *The Chosen* by CHAIM POTOK

The insightful story of the friendship between two Jewish boys, one Orthodox and the other Hasidic, who grow up in Brooklyn in the waning years of World War II, trying to define their religious, political, and intellectual beliefs.

3 *The Brief Wondrous Life of Oscar Wao* by JUNOT DÍAZ

At the center of this novel about a superstitious Dominican family in New Jersey is Oscar Wao, a homely nerd who is obsessed with science fiction, comics, and finding love.

4 *Pachinko* by MIN JIN LEE

A Korean family living in Japan perseveres through generations of poverty, racial oppression, health challenges, and familial heartache.

5 *Family Life* by AKHIL SHARMA

When his family moves from India to New York and his brother suffers a brain injury that consumes his parents' attention, young Ajay Mishra works to find his own value and voice in an upside-down world.

6 *Fruit of the Drunken Tree* by INGRID ROJAS CONTRERAS

Chula, the sheltered daughter of a wealthy family living in a gated community in war-torn Bogotá, Colombia, becomes friends with the family's new live-in housemaid, Petrona, whose efforts to support her refugee family create extreme internal conflict and external danger for both girls.

7 *The Neighborhood* by MARIO VARGAS LLOSA

A crime thriller about elitist privilege, blackmail, extramarital affairs, murder, and corruption during the dark years of the Fujimori regime in Lima, Peru.

8 *Like Water for Chocolate* by LAURA ESQUIVEL

A novel set at the turn of the twentieth century in Mexico telling the story of how Tita De la Garza, the youngest daughter in her family, learns to offer love and wisdom through food.

9 *In a Free State* by V.S. NAIPAUL

A trio of short stories that use analogy to examine the price of freedom.

10 *Lost Children Archive* by VALERIA LUISELLI

An American family's cross-country trek involves them in the immigration crisis and heartbreaking encounters with refugee children that threaten the family's own sense of calling and identity.

11 *Invisible Man* by RALPH ELLISON

A nameless black protagonist attempts to escape the racism of the 1930s South by moving to New York, only to find that a different form of racism prevails in the North as well.

12 *Giovanni's Room* by JAMES BALDWIN

While his girlfriend is away in Spain preparing for their marriage, David, an American man living in Paris, meets and moves in with his Italian lover Giovanni. An early novel depicting the heartaches of bisexuality, gender identity, and the societal constructs of masculinity.

13 *Wizard of the Crow* by NGŨGĨ WA THIONG'O

A masterpiece of magical realism set in the fictional Free Republic of Aburiria, where the protagonists engage in a battle to overthrow their megalomaniac ruler.

14 *Kiss of the Spider Woman* by MANUEL PUIG

Two very different inmates in an Argentine prison, Molina (a middle-aged gay man) and Valentin (a young socialist revolutionary), form an unlikely, life-changing bond through conversation and Molina's recountings of his favorite films.

15 *On Earth We're Briefly Gorgeous* by OCEAN VUONG

An epistolary novel written by a Vietnamese-American son, Little Dog, to his illiterate mother, processing the family's tragic history and exploring the pursuit of life and joy beyond mere survival.

16 *The Stationery Shop* by MARJAN KAMALI

Set in 1953 Tehran, this is the story of two Iranian lovers who first meet and fall in love in the neighborhood book and stationery shop, are separated by a violent political uprising on the night before their wedding, and meet again by chance sixty years later in America.

17 *Zipper Mouth* by LAURIE WEEKS

The exquisite torture of unrequited love as felt by a young, drug-addicted lesbian woman trying to find her way in New York City.

18 *When We Left Cuba* by CHANEL CLEETON

After her family is forced to flee Cuba and resettle in Florida, Beatriz Perez's love for her Cuban homeland and her hatred for Castro results in her involvement in CIA intrigues leading up to the Bay of Pigs. There are also several marriage proposals along the way in this combination love story and realistic account of Cuban history.

19 *2666* by ROBERTO BOLAÑO

Set in the fictional Mexican border town of Santa Teresa, this epic novel brings together a disparate cast of characters to investigate the unsolved murders of hundreds of young women in Santa Teresa.

20 *The Air You Breathe* by FRANCES DE PONTES PEEBLES

An exploration of the complexities of female friendship, this novel follows the intertwined lives and relationship between two girls in 1930s Brazil—Dores, an orphan working in the kitchen of a sugar cane plantation, and

Graça, the privileged daughter of a wealthy family, both drawn to the world of samba music and dance.

21 *The Book of Salt* by MONIQUE TRUONG

Binh, a Vietnamese cook exiled from his native land because of his homosexuality, works for two wealthy expatriate Americans in Paris—Gertrude Stein and Alice B. Toklas—while attempting to find himself and love, and heal from the wounds of growing up in a colonial society.

22 *The White Tiger* by ARAVIND ADIGA

Written to give a voice to India's impoverished lower class, this novel details village boy Balram's lifelong battle with, and ultimate triumph over, the Indian caste system.

23 *1Q84* by HARUKI MURAKAMI

Mystery, dystopia, and romance are fused together in the converging story lines of two characters: Aomame, an assassin who finds herself transported into an alternate world while on the way to an appointment in Tokyo, and Tengo, an aspiring writer.

24 *Taipei* by TAO LIN

Paul, a successful yet bored and anxious young novelist, battles escalating addictions to online media and to drugs that repeatedly sabotage his romantic relationships.

25 *A Brief History of Seven Killings* by MARLON JAMES

Chronicling the upheaval and violence that swirled through Jamaica in the 1970s and 1980s, the story opens with the attempted murder of reggae superstar Bob Marley, and expands from there into an exploration of race, class, poverty, and the temperamental relationship between Jamaica and the US.

26 *What Belongs to You* by GARTH GREENWELL

In this novel set in contemporary Bulgaria, two gay lovers discover how desire and violence merge into both ecstasy and anguish, and how cultural history shapes our own stories.

27 *Ghachar Ghochar* by VIVEK SHANBHAG

When their fortunes improve overnight, a once-close family in Bangalore begins to fall apart under the new tensions and pressures introduced by money. A study in contemporary Indian culture and in human nature.

28 *A Place for Us* by FATIMA FARHEEN MIRZA

Three siblings endeavor to honor the Indian culture and religion of their Muslim parents while embracing their own paths and identities in America.

29 *Akata Witch* by NNEDI OKORAFOR

Twelve-year-old Sunny is an albino witch born in New York who struggles to find her place in her new Nigerian home until she becomes friends with Orlu and Chichi and meets the Leopard People.

30 *The Parking Lot Attendant* by NAFKOTE TAMIRAT

A father and his seventeen-year-old daughter seek refuge in a commune on a subtropical island, where they get entangled in a web of intrigue when the manipulative community leader turns his attention to the daughter.

BOOK CLUB FAVORITES

1 *All the Light We Cannot See* by ANTHONY DOERR

Fate weaves together the lives of a blind French girl and a German orphan boy as they struggle for life and hope in World War II Europe.

2 *The Water Dancer* by TA-NEHISI COATES

Hiram's unique magical power, bestowed on him when his enslaved mother was taken away from him, gives him courage to seek out a new life for himself and to become involved in the Underground Railroad, rescuing other slaves and conducting them to freedom.

3 *Little Fires Everywhere* by CELESTE NG

In Shaker Heights, a peaceful and ordered suburb of Cleveland, an entire neighborhood suffers when the children of nearby families become friends but their mothers become estranged.

4 *The Farm* by JOANNE RAMOS

Imaginative and thought-provoking, this novel recounts the story of four women who are promised a handsome fee to be surrogates for wealthy couples. It explores the ethics surrounding surrogacy in a way that is anything but academic or philosophical.

5 *Three Things About Elsie* by JOANNA CANNON

A mystery involving the reappearance of a dead man (or his perfect look-alike), a six-decade friendship, and the quirks of the elderly. A beautiful story about relationships and redemption.

6 *The World That We Knew* by ALICE HOFFMAN

A mystical spirit guide created by a mother's love shepherds two Jewish girls during their desperate escape from Berlin to France in 1941.

7 *The Underground Railroad* by COLSON WHITEHEAD

Combining elements of history and fantasy, this winner of the 2017 Pulitzer Prize tells the unforgettable story of Cora, a third-generation Georgia slave who escapes to freedom via a real network of underground tunnels.

8 *The Lost Queen* by SIGNE PIKE

A historical fantasy set in sixth-century Celtic Britain whose heroine is Languoreth, a queen who fights to save the druid ways of her kingdom from the encroachment of Christian evangelists and Anglo-Saxons. Nearly unlimited discussion potential on issues as relevant today as they are in their historical setting.

9 *A Man Called Ove* by FREDRIK BACKMAN

The life of a crotchety old man is turned upside-down when a loud and lively family moves in next door. Turns out, it might just be what the whole neighborhood needed.

10 *The Line of Beauty* by ALAN HOLLINGHURST

Exploring themes of mental health, hypocrisy, privilege, and homosexuality, this story centers on young, gay protagonist Nick Guest who helps stabilize the daughter of wealthy conservatives who offer him a place to live but don't welcome his lifestyle.

11 *Finding Dorothy* by ELIZABETH LETTS

This delightfully imaginative backstory to L. Frank Baum's classic, *The Wonderful Wizard of Oz*, explores the friendship between Baum's wife, Maud, and young Dorothy—both the real-life girl who inspired the character and the actress who plays the character, Judy Garland.

12 *All Grown Up* by JAMI ATTENBERG

All of Andrea's attempts to distance herself from her troubled past and ignore her own personal issues begin to fall apart when her niece Sigrid is born.

13 *Good Omens: The Nice and Accurate Prophecies of Agnes Nutter, Witch* by TERRY PRATCHETT AND NEIL GAIMAN

An angel and a demon, hereditary enemies, become friends and fall in love with the world of humans. When Armageddon threatens, they band together to save the earth.

14 *Things You Save in a Fire* by KATHERINE CENTER

Cassie is a fierce Texas firefighter who's an expert at dealing with other people's emergencies, but her move to Boston to care for her sick mother throws change and uncertainty over everything, including her resolute avoidance of romantic relationships—especially those with firefighters.

15 *Good Luck with That* by KRISTAN HIGGINS

Emerson's dying wish for her two best friends is that they move toward conquering their fears. In the process of honoring Emerson's request, Marley and Georgia learn about loving themselves.

16 *The Dutch House* by ANN PATCHETT

Their parents gone and their family home taken from them, Danny and Maeve share a sibling bond that enabled them to survive their painful past but now shackles them to each other. Could it truncate their futures?

17 *Patsy* by NICOLE DENNIS-BENN

Patsy longs for freedom to be herself and to be united with her longtime friend and former lover, Cicely, in the US. When she leaves her daughter Tru behind in Jamaica to immigrate to America, she sets in motion a chain of events that will unfold for many years before mother and daughter find each other again.

18 *Circe* by MADELINE MILLER

Circe is the daughter of the sun god, Helios, and the ocean nymph, Perse, but has powers that are different from those of the other gods. As she discovers and hones her own secret gifts, she also grows attached to mortals. One day, she will have to choose where to cast her lot.

19 *The Ensemble* by AJA GABEL

The power of music to draw people together and forge enduring friendship shines brightly in the story of Jana, Brit, Daniel, and Henry, four friends who are members of a string quartet.

20 *Shadow Child* by RAHNA REIKO RIZZUTO

In this suspenseful psychological novel set in Hawaii, New York, and Japan, Hana and Kei, twin sisters with a mixed-race heritage, are inseparable until the death of their mother and a subsequent betrayal that drives them apart. Will they choose to believe in second chances?

21 *Self-Portrait with Boy* by RACHEL LYON

When Lu Rile, a struggling, ambitious young artist, accidentally captures the image of a tragedy in the background of a photo, she is faced with the choice of monetizing her picture or protecting those affected by the tragedy.

22 *Everyone Knows You Go Home* by NATALIA SYLVESTER

The ghost of Isabel's father-in-law, Omar, comes back year after year on the Day of the Dead to plead for a chance at forgiveness and redemption, but only Isabel can see him.

23 *Oliver Loving* by STEFAN MERRILL BLOCK

A shooting at a Texas high school dance leaves shy Oliver Loving brain-damaged, paralyzed, and mute, though he is the only one who knows exactly what happened that night. Ten years later, a medical breakthrough may give Oliver back his voice and provide answers to all the lingering questions about the tragic event.

24 *The Friend* by SIGRID NUNEZ

When a woman inherits a Great Dane upon the death of its owner and her lifelong best friend, she nearly loses her own life and sanity in order to bond with and care for the dog.

25 *Things Fall Apart* by CHINUA ACHEBE

The inevitable culture clash that comes when European colonization and Western religion (in the form of missionaries) flood Okonkwo's traditional Nigerian village.

26 *In the Shadow of 10,000 Hills* by JENNIFER HAUPT

Three women, each on a separate personal quest for answers and grace, find their stories intersecting in post-genocide Rwanda.

27 *Census* by JESSE BALL

A single father with a terminal illness takes a final road trip as a census taker, searching for a home for his beloved adult son with Down syndrome.

28 *Stray City* by CHELSEY JOHNSON

Andrea Morales is a young artist who escaped her traditional Midwestern family and joined a tight-knit lesbian community in Portland, Oregon. When she becomes pregnant and decides to keep the baby, the circle of friends that had banded together to support each other strains to care for her.

29 *The Wild Birds* by EMILY STRELOW

A silver box of eggshells ties together three distinct survival narratives from the American northwest over the course of a century.

30 *Celine* by PETER HELLER

In this detective novel set in Brooklyn and the American west, Celine is a sixty-eight-year-old private investigator who is better than the FBI at solving mysteries, but Gabriela's plea for help in finding out the truth about her missing father pulls Celine into the darkest case she's ever known.

TIMELESS YOUNG ADULT LITERATURE

1 *The Hate U Give* by ANGIE THOMAS

Narrated from the perspective of Starr Carter, a teenage girl who is split between her poor community and her upper-class prep school, this novel targets racial and social injustice, and the human need for belonging and family.

2 *The Fault in Our Stars* by JOHN GREEN

Hazel, a sixteen-year-old with terminal cancer, falls in love with Augustus, a seventeen-year-old whose cancer is in remission. Is their love enough to heal Hazel?

3 ***The Witch of Blackbird Pond*** by ELIZABETH GEORGE SPEARE

When her beloved grandfather dies, orphaned Kit Tyler leaves the Caribbean and boards a ship to New England to try to find an aunt she's never met and establish a new home. But her Puritan community treats the new arrival with great suspicion, especially after she strikes up a friendship with the witch of Blackbird Pond.

4 ***The Book Thief*** by MARKUS ZUSAK

In 1939 Nazi Germany, little Liesel's world centers around two things: reading her stolen books and finding out about the young Jewish man hiding in her foster family's cellar.

5 ***The Call of the Wild*** by JACK LONDON

Buck is a remarkably powerful but domesticated dog who is stolen from his owner and taken to the Alaskan wilderness, where he learns to fight for his survival in both the civilized world and the wild.

6 ***The Giver*** by LOIS LOWRY

In a futuristic dystopian society that is as empty of color as it is of emotion, young Jonas is chosen to be the next keeper of the community's memories. It's a unique role with unique burdens, and Jonas begins to envision a different future for his community.

7 ***The Catcher in the Rye*** by J.D. SALINGER

Holden Caulfield, an intelligent yet jaded teenager recently expelled from his prep school, sets out on a self-imposed mission to find meaningful connections and to protect himself and other children from losing their innocence.

8 ***Speak*** by LAURIE HALSE ANDERSON

Melinda loses her voice and much of her former life after being raped at a high school party. Her lab partner David eventually helps her fight back and speak up for herself again.

9 ***The Perks of Being a Wallflower*** by STEPHEN CHBOSKY

In this coming-of-age novel told in a series of letters, Charlie periodically experiences flashbacks of his aunt Helen, which seem unrelated to the rest of his life until he expresses his love for longtime friend and crush, Sam. That's when the memories come flooding back.

10 *The House on Mango Street* by SANDRA CISNEROS

Escaping from her hated life on Mango Street, a Latino neighborhood in Chicago, is Esperanza's main goal, but her friend's aunts, the Three Sisters, teach her to own her life and story with compassion.

11 *The Absolutely True Diary of a Part-Time Indian* by SHERMAN ALEXIE

Instead of remaining at a troubled school on the Spokane Indian Reservation, aspiring cartoonist Junior chooses to attend an all-white, off-reservation high school to escape his family's legacy of alcoholism and poverty.

12 *Lies We Tell Ourselves* by ROBIN TALLEY

Two high school girls on opposing sides of the school integration battle in 1959 Virginia are assigned to be school project partners, forcing them to examine the racial lies and cultural expectations they've accepted their whole lives.

13 *Dumplin'* by JULIE MURPHY

Willowdean Dickson, the daughter of a teen beauty queen, has always been secure in her own body and self-image even though she's overweight. Meeting handsome Bo changes all of that and erodes her self-confidence, so she enters a beauty pageant to prove that she doesn't need to be thin to succeed at the pageant and at life.

14 *The Girl from Everywhere* by HEIDI HEILIG

If there's a map, her father's magic ship can go there: any time, any world. Nix grew up sailing through galaxies, millennia, and imagination, but her father's next voyage might unmake her.

15 *Roll of Thunder, Hear My Cry* by MILDRED D. TAYLOR

Cassie is only nine years old, but she already has to face the brutal realities of what it means to be part of a black family in Mississippi during the Great Depression. As tragedy and injustice strike, Cassie looks to the skies for help.

16 *Watership Down* by RICHARD ADAMS

A tale full of charm and high adventure about a rabbit clan's pilgrimage to flee the humans who are encroaching on their warren and find a new home in the downs of southern England.

17 *A Day No Pigs Would Die* by ROBERT NEWTON PECK

Robert plays hooky from school one day and ends up with a new pet, a piglet named Pinky, who becomes his best friend and helps him weather the trials ahead.

18 *Stargirl* by JERRY SPINELLI

A quirky homeschooler enrolls in tenth grade at Mica High. She's weird, yet somehow winsome, and her presence slowly brings a fresh perspective to her classmates and friends.

19 *The Outsiders* by S.E. HINTON

In Tulsa, Oklahoma, in the 1960s, a teenage-gang conflict escalates into a citywide brawl that changes the town and the lives of the gang members forever.

20 *Are You There God? It's Me, Margaret.* by JUDY BLUME

Margaret Simon, who's recently moved from New York City to suburban New Jersey, doesn't have a religion like most of her friends do, but she does have her own way of talking to God.

21 **The Hunger Games Trilogy** by SUZANNE COLLINS

In a dystopian world that pits children against each other in gladiator-like fights to the death, Katniss and Peeta have the courage and ingenuity to fight back against the system.

22 *More Happy Than Not* by ADAM SILVERA

Aaron's unhappy memories and his emerging sexual identity aren't welcome on his block. He wonders if undergoing the memory-changing experiments at the Leteo Institute will help him.

23 *Patron Saints of Nothing* by RANDY RIBAY

Filipino-American teenager Jay Reguero is disturbed by the silence and mystery surrounding his Filipino cousin's death, so he travels to the Philippines to search for the truth.

24 *Internment* by SAMIRA AHMED

In an alternate reality (that strikes a little too close to home), teenager Layla Amin and her Muslim friends are placed in concentration camps as Islamophobia washes over the nation.

25 *The Thief* by MEGAN WHALEN TURNER

Gen is an imprisoned criminal, but the magus finds his thievery skills useful and decides to put him to work on an official mission full of danger and intrigue.

26 *The Female of the Species* by MINDY MCGINNIS

After the rape and murder of her older sister, Alex Craft took her revenge on the killer and then isolated herself in her own private world. Despite her remoteness, though, Peekay and Jack slowly befriend her, and her dark side breaks out and sets all three teenagers careening toward disaster.

27 *The Truth About Forever* by SARAH DESSEN

Since her father's death, Macy's world has gotten smaller and smaller until she takes a job with a catering company and makes friends with Wes, breaking it wide open again.

28 *The Lion, the Witch and the Wardrobe* by C.S. LEWIS

Sent out of London during World War II to live with a professor in an old country house, the four Pevensie children stumble into a wardrobe and find themselves transported to the magical kingdom of Narnia.

29 *The Curious Incident of the Dog in the Night-Time* by MARK HADDON

Christopher, a mathematically gifted autistic fifteen-year-old, decides to chronicle his investigation into what happened to the dog he found dead in his neighbor's yard.

30 *Ghost* by JASON REYNOLDS

Castle Cranshaw, nicknamed "Ghost," is running from the demons in his life but wants to join the local elite track team. Will Coach give him a chance?

MEMOIRS

1 *The Gentrification of the Mind: Witness to a Lost Imagination* by SARAH SCHULMAN

Schulman reflects on her experience of the AIDS crisis in New York City, and wrestles with the devastating and deadening effects of a gentrification that excludes minorities from far more than just affordable housing.

2 *Almost a Woman* by ESMERALDA SANTIAGO

In this sequel to her memoir *When I Was Puerto Rican,* Santiago recounts her teenage years growing up in the tenements of Brooklyn in a supportive but restrictive family, and her entrance into the world of the arts and acting.

3 *Bird of Paradise: How I Became Latina* by RAQUEL CEPEDA

Raquel Cepeda recounts how she grew up in New York City and Santo Domingo, being passed around between relatives and fending for herself on neighborhood streets and in schools, yet emerging from her stressful childhood to become a journalist and documentary filmmaker intent on reconnecting with her roots.

4 *The Best We Could Do* by THI BUI

Cartoonist Thi Bui's graphic memoir of a Vietnamese family's flight from their war-torn country in search of hope and a new life.

5 *Educated* by TARA WESTOVER

In this insightful memoir, Westover describes overcoming her survivalist Mormon family as well as her complete lack of formal schooling to go to college and eventually earn her PhD from Cambridge University.

6 *Priestdaddy: A Memoir* by PATRICIA LOCKWOOD

When Lockwood and her husband have to move in with her parents due to an unexpected health crisis, her new life and her old fundamentalist Catholic roots—in particular, her Catholic priest father—collide.

7 *The Color of Water: A Black Man's Tribute to His White Mother*
by JAMES MCBRIDE

McBride's paean to his mother, offering the perspective of a black man raised
by a white mom in the all-black public housing projects of Red Hook, Brooklyn.

8 *All You Can Ever Know* by NICOLE CHUNG

Adopted by a white Catholic family in Oregon when she was two months
old, Chung began the search for her biological Korean family when she
found out she was expecting a child of her own.

9 *Everything Happens for a Reason: And Other Lies I've Loved* by
KATE BOWLER

A historian at Duke Divinity School, Bowler is forced to reexamine her faith
after being diagnosed with stage IV cancer in her early thirties.

10 *I Am, I Am, I Am: Seventeen Brushes with Death* by MAGGIE
O'FARRELL

How the seventeen near-death situations that Northern Irish novelist Maggie O'Farrell has lived through have profoundly defined and shaped her life.

11 *Stitches* by DAVID SMALL

Children's author and illustrator David Small recounts his sickly childhood, the scarring surgery that his parents put him through without any
preparation and little or no compassion, his escape through his art, and his
pursuit of professional help and healing.

12 *You All Grow Up and Leave Me: A Memoir of Teenage Obsession*
by PIPER WEISS

Weiss's reflections on the conflicted and compromising relationship she
had with her tennis coach, exploring the lingering effects of a predator's
sexual grooming of vulnerable children.

13 *Heart Berries* by TERESE MARIE MAILHOT

Mailhot emerged from a traumatic childhood on an Indian Reservation
in the Pacific Northwest, only to find herself hospitalized with PTSD and
bipolar disorder. She shares her courageous journey toward connection
and reintegration here.

14 *Glitter and Glue* by KELLY CORRIGAN

In this memoir about the many-layered relationship between a mother and a daughter, Corrigan recounts how her adversarial relationship with her pragmatic mom started to change when Corrigan became a live-in nanny and had to care for kids of her own.

15 *When a Crocodile Eats the Sun* by PETER GODWIN

A portrait of personal and national grief that weaves together the death of Godwin's father and the concurrent collapse of the Zimbabwean economy under Mugabe's dictatorship.

16 *Ordinary Girls* by JAQUIRA DÍAZ

The story of a journey from despair to rising hope in which Díaz recounts the challenges of growing up between the worlds of Puerto Rico and Miami Beach, with a mom battling mental illness amid a culture of violence and assault.

17 *From Scratch: A Memoir of Love, Sicily, and Finding Home* by
TEMBI LOCKE

After her husband's death, actress Tembi Locke and her daughter spend three summers in Sicily with his family, where Tembi receives physical and spiritual healing sitting at her mother-in-law's table.

18 *The World According to Fannie Davis* by BRIDGETT M. DAVIS

A daughter's account of her larger-than-life mother and the secret empire of generosity and compassion that she built.

19 *Choose Your Own Disaster* by DANA SCHWARTZ

Schwartz's feminist millennial manifesto is written in the form of a long personality quiz that tells the story of her hilarious and sometimes heart-breakingly relatable journey to come into her own.

20 *Out of Egypt* by ANDRÉ ACIMAN

Aciman recalls his Jewish childhood in Alexandria in a family that was chock-full of colorful characters and eccentric geniuses, conjuring up the treasured past that deeply informed his present.

MEMOIRS, CONTINUED

21 *The Diving Bell and the Butterfly* by JEAN-DOMINIQUE BAUBY

Written one blink at a time, this is a journalist's memoir of life after a stroke left him, at forty-three years old, paralyzed and able to control only the muscles of his left eye.

22 *Yes, Chef* by MARCUS SAMUELSSON

An acclaimed chef recounts how his love for food and cooking in his adopted grandmother's kitchen launched him on a journey from her family table to his own world-renowned restaurants.

23 *I Know Why the Caged Bird Sings* by MAYA ANGELOU

In Maya Angelou's poetic memoir detailing her unstable and traumatic childhood between the ages of three to sixteen, her indomitable spirit triumphs over tragedy.

24 *The Woman Warrior* by MAXINE HONG KINGSTON

In a memoir that combines autobiography, Chinese folk tales, and her own mother's "talk-stories," a Chinese-American daughter learns to fight for wholeness with the wisdom of words: her own words and the interwoven words of the women in her life.

25 *This Boy's Life* by TOBIAS WOLFF

In Wolff's anguished upbringing, he was abandoned by his father, cut off from his brother, and raised by a mother with violent boyfriends who tormented Wolff. In the process, Tobias reinvents himself as "Jack" and tries to cling to his dreams, escaping through his imagination and attempts at self-creation.

26 *Autobiography of a Face* by LUCY GREALY

This harrowing and beautifully written autobiography tells the story of Lucy Grealy, who at nine years old endured agonizing treatments for jaw cancer and surgery that disfigured her face.

27 *Becoming* by MICHELLE OBAMA

From her roots in Chicago's South Side to college at Princeton, law school at Harvard, and finally to the White House and beyond, one of America's most inspiring leaders tells her story.

28 *Angela's Ashes: A Memoir* by **FRANK MCCOURT**

Written with wry humor that belies his bleak childhood, this Pulitzer Prize–winning memoir details McCourt's boyhood as the son of poor Irish parents in New York, growing up in poverty and taking care of three younger brothers, yet nurturing a dream of returning to the land of his birth.

29 *A Heartbreaking Work of Staggering Genius* by **DAVE EGGERS**

At twenty-one, the author is forced to be a single parent when the sudden death of both of his parents from cancer leaves him with custody of his eight-year-old brother.

30 *Me Talk Pretty One Day* by **DAVID SEDARIS**

A compilation of amusing personal essays full of commentary on life from a gay traveler, writer, and humorist.

OTHER BOOKS I'D LIKE TO READ

1 .... *TITLE* ☐

   by .... *AUTHOR*

2 .... ☐

   by ....

3 .... ☐

   by ....

4 .... ☐

   by ....

5 .... ☐

   by ....

6 .... ☐

   by ....

7 .... ☐

   by ....

8 .... ☐

   by ....

9 .... ☐

   by ....

10 .... ☐

   by ....

11 .... ☐

   by ....

12 .... ☐

   by ....

13 .... ☐

   by ....

14 .... ☐

   by ....

15 .... ☐

   by ....

16 .... ☐

by ....

17 .... ☐

by ....

18 .... ☐

by ....

19 .... ☐

by ....

20 .... ☐

by ....

21 .... ☐

by ....

22 .... ☐

by ....

23 .... ☐

by ....

24 .... ☐

by ....

25 .... ☐

by ....

26 .... ☐

by ....

27 .... ☐

by ....

28 .... ☐

by ....

29 .... ☐

by ....

30 .... ☐

by ....

SAMPLE DISCUSSION QUESTIONS

1   What one word would you use to describe the book?

2   Does the opening scene foreshadow themes or events throughout the rest of the story?

3   What was the dominant emotion you felt as you walked away from the book?

4   Do you think the title fits the work?

5   Which character changed the most throughout the course of the story?

6   Are there loose ends that you wish were tied up?

7   What was the main message or idea that the author wanted to communicate through the work?

8   Did the subplots support or distract from the main plot?

9   If the author wrote a sequel, what would you want the sequel to be about? Who should be the main character in the sequel?

10   Who would you want to share this book with and why?

11   How important is the time period and setting to the plot of the book?

12   Does the writing style enhance or detract from the reading experience?

13 If you didn't like the book and didn't finish it, what made you give up on it?

14 If you didn't like the book but finished it anyway, why did you persevere?

15 What were the main values presented in the story? Do you agree or disagree with these values?

16 How were events in the book structured?

17 Was the plot development linear or fragmented?

18 Which character do you think reflected the author's point of view most consistently?

19 Which events or dialogues serve as turning points in the story?

20 Was the dialogue realistic and well developed?

21 If you were casting the book for a movie, which actors would you choose to be the main characters?

22 Did the book match your expectations?

23 What is the most important relationship in the book?

24 Share a favorite quote or a moment from the book that touched you. Why was it significant to you?

25 What was original or unique about the book?

26 How would the story change if the protagonist had a different gender?

27 Which character did you identify with the most and why?

28 Did the book influence your perspective or change your mind about anything?

29 What other books would you compare with this work?

30 Are you interested in reading other books by this author?

31 If you could insert yourself into this book, who/what/where/when/how would you want to be?

32 Were there any noticeable holes or inconsistencies in the plot or in the world-building?

33 What was there too little of?

34 What was there too much of?

35 What was just right?

36 Which character would you most want to meet?

37 Is there anything you still feel confused about?

38 Which characters and events didn't feel believable?

39 If you could design the cover, how would you envision it?

40 Would you read this book again? What would you want to revisit?

41 Did you primarily agree or disagree with the viewpoint and agenda of the author?

42 What metaphors or symbols show up throughout the book?

43 Did the book bring up any personal memories for you?

44 What surprised you along the way? What didn't you see coming?

45 If this book were recast in a different genre, what genre would that be?

46 What is your one-sentence summary of the book?

47 If you could change one thing about the book, what would it be?

48 Were there any parts of the book that made you uncomfortable or struck you as inappropriate?

49 Is the book plot-driven or character-driven?

50 Do you think you could be good friends with the author?